# MARGINAL
# OPERATION

**AUTHOR**
## Yuri Shibamura

Marginal Operation
Seikaisha Fictions

**ILLUSTRATOR**
## Daisuke Kimura

**SETTING ASSISTANCE**
## Shizuma Yoshinori

# M.O.05

STORY BY YURI SHIBAMURA
MANGA BY DAISUKE KIMURA

# M.O.05
## CONTENTS

SIGN: PORORI PARK PEDESTRIAN ENTRANCE - KAWASAKI PORT AND HARBOR AUTHORITY

ぽろり公園
歩行者
入口
川崎市港湾局

OPERATION_024
**SORTIE**

10:41
Room1
94%

Join channel

ピ
BEEP

IT'S
ALMOST
TIME...

TACTICAL UNIT SA IS IN POSITION.

TACTICAL UNIT SC, IN POSITION.

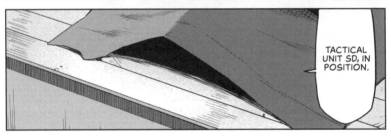

TACTICAL UNIT SD, IN POSITION.

TACTICAL UNIT SE REPORTING IN. PEOPLE STARTED ARRIVING AFTER SUNRISE.

THEY APPEAR TO BE WAREHOUSE WORKERS.

IBN, YOU AND YOUR SQUAD CAN TAKE A BREAK.

SQUAD SD WILL TAKE OVER SURVEILLANCE.

WHAT'S UP?

OMAR.

ARATA...

DON'T TELL ME YOU SECRETLY SNUCK CAMERAS ON US OR SOMETHING.

YOUR CURRENT LOCATION ISN'T HALF-BAD, BUT YOU'LL START ATTRACTING ATTENTION ONCE THE PLACE GETS MORE CROWDED.

I IMAGINE YOU'RE ALREADY ADJUSTING YOUR LOCATION TO ACCOMMODATE FOR THE SUN'S POSITION, BUT CAN YOU MOVE FORWARD ANOTHER HUNDRED METERS? I WANT YOU UNDER THE BRIDGE.

I'M JUST USING MY IMAGINATION, LIKE USUAL.

OF COURSE NOT.

NO PROBLEM.

NOW THEN...

ROGER. WELL, I WAS WORRIED WE MIGHT BE TOO CONSPICUOUS HERE.

SO THANKS FOR THE HEADS UP.

6

GUESS I'LL DIRECT THE OPERATION FROM THIS PARK.

BARK! BARK!

THIS PLACE SEEMS PRETTY BUSY,

ESPECIALLY FOR A WEEKDAY.

THOUGH, I'VE GOTTA SAY...

Ah!

BUMP

I'M NOT THE ONLY MIDDLE-AGED GUY AROUND HERE, SO I WON'T STICK OUT.

WELL, IT'S PROBABLY NOT A BIG DEAL.

AH...

S—

SORRY.

WHOA...

HE'S SCARY...

...TREMBLE

YOU IN THE MIDDLE OF WORK THERE, BRO-THER?

HEH! NO NEED TO LOOK SO SCARED, HE WON'T BITE.

LICK

....

SORRY ABOUT THAT, BROTHER! HEY, APOLO-GIZE FOR BUMPING INTO THE YOUNG MAN!

AHA-HAHA!

CHATTER

CHATTER

GOD'S ALWAYS WATCHING OVER US, WHEREVER WE ARE.

IT'S THE SAME NO MATTER WHERE WE GO.

A YEAR OUT, AND I STILL END UP RELYING ON THE KIDS TO FIGHT.

IN THE END, NOTHING'S CHANGED.

I NEED TO GET A GRIP.

WE'RE IN THE MIDDLE OF AN OPERATION HERE. IF I HAVE TIME TO BROOD, I HAVE TIME TO VISUALIZE A BETTER STRATEGY.

SCRATCH SCRATCH

I DON'T DESERVE TO BE CALLED A HEAD-MASTER.

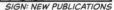

SIGN: NEW PUBLICATIONS

COME ON, THINK!

IMAGINE WHAT THE KIDS' BATTLE-FIELD LOOKS LIKE.

PICTURE HOW THEY'LL FIGHT, AND WHERE.

THAT'S HOW YOU CAN PROTECT THEM.

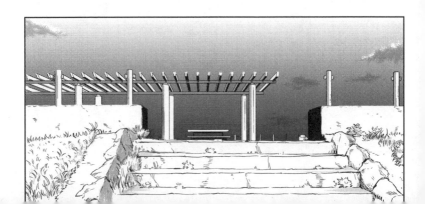

IBN, ARE YOU AWAKE?

YES, SIR.

ROGER.

WE JUST NEED THE MOLOTOVS TO HIT THE GENERAL VICINITY OF OUR TARGET.

DON'T WORRY TOO MUCH ABOUT ACCURACY WHEN YOU START THROWING.

MESS

EVEN I WOULDN'T COME UP WITH A TRAP THAT LEAVES US SO OPEN... I THINK THEY'RE ACTUALLY THAT INCOMPETENT.

BUT JUST IN CASE, CONTINUE MONITORING THE SITUATION.

DO YOU THINK IT'S A TRAP?

NO. THEY HAVEN'T EVEN POSTED SNIPERS.

JINI, HAVE THERE BEEN ANY ENEMY MOVEMENTS?

!!

JIBRIL REPORTING. OUR INTEL WAS ACCURATE, THE TRUCK HAS ARRIVED.

IT'S ALONE.

RUMBLE

POINT

TRUCK: "LOYALTY"

BE CAREFUL OUT THERE.

VERY WELL. LET'S GO WITH PLAN 1-1. INFORM THE OTHERS.

WAVE WAVE

ROGER.

SIP

NO, WE'RE GOING WITH PLAN 1-1.

SERI-OUSLY...

I WAS TOLD THAT WE'RE EXECUTING PLAN 1-1... DID I MISHEAR?

OMAR REPORTING.

RATTLE

HOPEFULLY THIS OPERATION TEACHES THEM TO TAKE SECURITY MORE SERIOUSLY.

EITHER WAY, THIS IS GOOD FOR US.

AND THESE GUYS RUN A CRIME RING? HOW THE HELL HAVE THEY SURVIVED UNTIL NOW?

OUR ENEMY APPEARS TO BE MORE COMPLACENT THAN I EXPECTED.

I KNOW. BUT WE'RE ONLY FIGHTING THEM BECAUSE OUR JOB REQUIRES US TO.

WAVE WAVE

I DON'T THINK NOW'S THE TIME TO BE WORRYING ABOUT OUR OPPONENT'S WELL-BEING.

NO MATTER WHAT HAPPENS, THERE'S NO POINT IN HOLDING A GRUDGE.

ROGER.

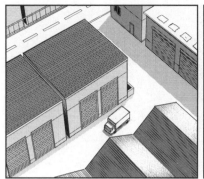

NOW THEN...

TAP

TAP

LET'S GET STARTED.

SO THERE WON'T BE ANY CROSSWIND INTERFERING WITH THE SQUAD'S ARROWS.

TWANG

THE WIND'S BLOWING SEAWARD...

WHOOSH

THWACK

THE WAREHOUSE ENTRANCE WILL CATCH FIRE.

ONCE THE GRENADES LAND...

I SEE.

SO THEY'VE CALLED THE DEAL OFF.

THEY'LL LIKELY HALT THE DEAL RIGHT AWAY. MAYBE THEY'LL EVEN SAY THOSE CHEESY LINES YOU ALWAYS HEAR IN HOLLYWOOD MOVIES.

CONSIDERING HOW CARELESS THIS CRIMINAL ORGANIZATION HAS BEEN SO FAR, THAT'LL BE ENOUGH TO SEND THEM INTO A PANIC.

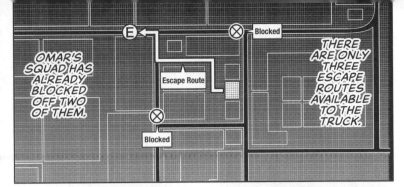

OMAR'S SQUAD HAS ALREADY BLOCKED OFF TWO OF THEM.

THERE ARE ONLY THREE ESCAPE ROUTES AVAILABLE TO THE TRUCK.

E

⊗ Blocked

Escape Route

⊗ Blocked

THEY'LL FIRE A VOLLEY OF CROSS-BOW BOLTS.

TWANG

TWANG

TWANG

ONCE THE ENEMY IS IN SIGHT,

SD ▶

E

SA ◀

WHERE JINI AND JIBRIL'S SQUADS WILL BE WAITING.

THE SMUGGLERS WILL BE FORCED TO TAKE THE ONE ROUTE WE'VE LEFT OPEN,

SHATTER

BOOM

TARGET NEUTRAL-IZED.

I GUESS THAT MEANS THE TRUCK MUST HAVE TOPPLED OVER.

THAT'S THE SECOND EXPLOSION...

BOOM

RATATA TATATA!

!!!

RUSTLE

USING THE KITCHEN KNIVES WE BOUGHT AS REPLACEMENTS FOR COMBAT ONES.

WHOOSH

JIBRIL'S SQUAD WILL ENSURE THERE ARE NO SURIVORS,

ENEMY ELIMINATED.

NONE OF THE SQUADS HAVE CONTACTED ME YET,

SO THE PLAN MUST STILL BE GOING SMOOTHLY.

THAT THIRD EXPLOSION WAS MUCH LOUDER THAN THE FIRST TWO.

WHICH MEANS THE THIRD EXPLOSION WAS JIBRIL'S SQUAD BLOWING UP THE VEHICLE THEY PILED ALL THE CORPSES INTO.

THEY PROBABLY HAD TO USE UP ALL OF THEIR REMAINING HAND GRENADES FOR THAT.

THE POLICE AND FIRE DEPARTMENTS WILL BE ARRIVING SOON.

WE NEED TO BEGIN OUR RETREAT. BUT FIRST...

I HOPE JINI MANAGED TO GET THE WEAPONS FROM THE TRUCK...

BEEP

I'LL SEND SQUAD SC AS BACK UP.

ROGER.

BEGIN FIRING IMMEDIATELY.

IBN HERE.

ROUGHLY HALF OF THE ENEMY'S FORCES HAVE RETREATED INTO THE WAREHOUSE.

STOMP

STOMP

STOMP

STOMP

OMAR!

STO

WE'RE ALMOST THERE!

DASH

!!!

ROGER!

MAKE SURE YOU ELIMINATE ALL ENEMIES.

THWACK TWACK

THWACK

THWACK THWACK

THW

ACK

OR MONEY, RIGHT?

ENEMY FORCES ELIMINATED.

SEARCH THE WAREHOUSE FOR ANY REMAINING WEAPONRY.

. . . . .

SO NOTHING USEFUL, HUH... DIDN'T THINK THEY'D BE TRADING WEAPONS FOR DRUGS.

DRUGS.

YOU'RE NOT GONNA LIKE WHAT WE JUST FOUND HERE...

HMM...

MIND IF I... COULD YOU... **BURN THEM TO ASH?**

MAKE SURE YOU DESTROY ALL THE SURVEILLANCE CAMERAS AS YOU LEAVE.

ONCE YOU'VE SET THE WARE-HOUSE AND THE BODIES ON FIRE, RUN TOWARD THE SEA. SNEAK UNDER THE HARBOR FENCE AND RETREAT FROM THERE.

*HAHAHA!* ROGER THAT!

HEH,

GOTCHA,

YEP! ME AND JIBRIL GOT OUT SAFE AND SOUND.

WHAT ABOUT THE OTHERS!?

ARE YOU OKAY!?

JINI REPORTING.

NO ONE'S GOT A SCRATCH ON THEM.

DON'T WORRY.

THANK GOODNESS.

24

I SEE. GOOD WORK YOU TWO.

THANKS...

WE GOT A BIG HAUL TOO!

THERE WERE SO MANY WEAPONS, I NEEDED JIBRIL'S HELP TO GET THEM ALL.

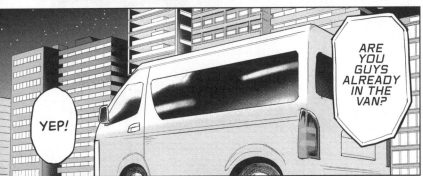

ARE YOU GUYS ALREADY IN THE VAN?

YEP!

SEE YOU ALL THERE.

I'LL START HEADING BACK TO THE INN THEN.

ROGER.

WELL...

APPARENTLY THERE'S BEEN AN INCIDENT AT KAWASAKI.

WHY THE LONG FACE?

SO...

ANYWAY...

PROBABLY.

IS THAT WHY EVERYONE IS GLUED TO THEIR PHONES?

I SEE...

HUH?

YEAH, WE GOT RID OF THEM ALL TOO.

DID YOU FIND THE DRUGS?

I SEE... WELL, LOOKS LIKE YOU'RE TRUST-WORTHY.

UMM... SO...

PLUS, UHH... I NEEDED SOMETHING FLAMMABLE TO CREMATE THE REMAINS, AND IT LOOKED LIKE THEY WOULD BURN WELL, SO...SORRY.

THE LAST THING I WANT IS ANY OF MY KIDS GETTING INVOLVED WITH DRUGS, SO WE DON'T DEAL IN STUFF LIKE THAT.

ERR...

THANKS.

WE BELIEVE YOU CAN SERVE JAPAN'S NATIONAL INTERESTS.

CONGRATULATIONS. YOU PASS.

SHE SURE IS IN A GOOD MOOD.

BOUNCE

BOUNCE

ニタ♪

ニタ♪

FIDGET

FIDGET

モジ

モジ

OR END UP TURNING INTO A NEW CRIMINAL ORGANIZATION.

I GUESS THEY'VE DECIDED WE WON'T BE A THREAT TO NATIONAL SECURITY,

DON'T WORRY, IT'LL BE MY TREAT!

IF YOU DON'T LIKE SUSHI, WE CAN DO SOMETHING ELSE, TOO.

DO YOU WANT TO GO GET SUSHI TO CELEBRATE!?

WHAT DO YOU SAY!?

HUH?

SORRY, BUT I'M AFRAID I'LL HAVE TO DECLINE.

AHAHA.

WHY IS SHE SO EXCITED?

ARE YOU IN THE MOOD FOR BBQ? WE CAN DO THAT INSTEAD!

THAT ASIDE...

FINE. I'LL JUST INVITE YOU SOME OTHER TIME.

.....

MY KIDS ARE WAITING FOR ME.

I WANT TO BE THERE TO WELCOME THEM.

THEN I'LL WAIT FOR THEM AT THE INN.

I SEE...

SINCE YOU'RE TAKING THE TRAIN BACK, YOU'LL RETURN WAY BEFORE THEY DO.

OH YEAH. THE INCIDENT AT KAWASAKI'S CAUSED TRAFFIC TO GET BACKED UP.

SIGNS: TSUBAMOTO INN

WE'RE BA—

THUD

ACK!

WELCOME BACK, EVERYONE.

DON'T OPEN THOSE OUT HERE!

H-HEY!

CHECK OUT ALL THE STUFF WE GOT!

I'M SOWWY.

SQUISH!

NEXT UP IS...

OKAY. WE'VE GOT OUR WEAP-ONS.

· · · · ·

BY A BUNCH OF KIDS USING CROSSBOWS, NO LESS!

GAHAHA! MAN, THOSE GUYS GOT STEAMROLLED!

NOW, NOW. THEY MIGHT HAVE STOLEN A FEW GUNS, BUT...

IF THEY'RE THIS GOOD, WE WON'T COME OUT OF A FIGHT UNSCATHED EITHER.

I'M SURE WE CAN FIND A WAY TO TURN THINGS AROUND.

32

OPERATION_025
# TARGET PRACTICE

AM I BEING PUNK'D RIGHT NOW?

I KNOW YOU SAID TO MEET YOU HERE, BUT...

YEAH, I DID...

TO THE SHOOTING RANGE, OF COURSE. DIDN'T YOU TELL ME YESTERDAY YOU NEEDED A PLACE TO CALIBRATE AND TEST YOUR WEAPONS?

HUH?

UMM... WHERE ARE YOU TAKING US?

DON'T WORRY, I'M A CERTIFIED TOUR GUIDE!

OR THAT YOU'D BE DRESSED LIKE THIS.

YOU'D HAVE A BUS WAITING...

I DIDN'T THINK

IT'LL PROBABLY BE FINE...

I THINK.

ERR...

UM...

I HAVE A BAD FEELING ABOUT THAT BUS.

ARATA...

ONJ TOURS FOR YOUR TRIP.

THANK YOU VERY MUCH FOR CHOOSING

PLEASE TAKE YOUR SEATS.

EVERY-ONE.

YOUR DRIVER TODAY WILL BE ONAGAWA.

I HOPE WE ALL CAN HAVE A FUN TIME TOGE-THER!

I'M STILL NEW TO THIS, BUT I PROMISE TO DO MY BEST.

......

AND I'LL BE YOUR GUIDE!

NOW THEN, I'D LIKE TO BEGIN BY GIVING YOU ALL A TOUR OF OUR LOVELY VEHICLE.

RAISE

NO THANK YOU.

THIS BUS IS EQUIPPED WITH RECLINING—

NO.

KA-THUNK

YOUR JOB'S PRETTY TOUGH, HUH...

TREMBLE    TREMBLE

THIS BUS—

NO.

KA-THUNK

MERRIM, LET HER TALK.

37

GOOD GRIEF.

I CAN'T BELIEVE ITOU-SAN.

THERE ARE PRIVATE SHOOTING RANGES LIKE THIS ONE IN THE COUNTRY.

THANK GOD

.....

WHEN SHE SHOWED UP WITH THAT BUS, I WAS WORRIED SHE WOULD TAKE US SOMEWHERE DANGEROUS, BUT...

IS THAT A CLONE OF THE M1911 COLT GOVERNMENT?

I HEARD IT'S CALLED THE M1911 BECAUSE IT WAS FIRST ADOPTED IN 1911.

THAT BEING SAID, DESPITE ADVANCEMENTS IN TECHNOLOGY, INFANTRY THESE DAYS HAVE IT HARDER THAN THEY USED TO.

IS THIS THE LIMIT OF HUMAN INGENUITY?

IT'S BEEN OVER A HUNDRED YEARS, BUT THIS IS STILL THE MOST COMMON PISTOL IN USE.

じっ…
STARE

THAT'S WHY MOST SQUADS NOWADAYS HAVE THINGS LIKE DONKEYS.

ANYWAY, THE POINT IS, MILITARY EQUIPMENT IS TOO HEAVY FOR KIDS TO BE CARRYING AROUND EVERYWHERE.

AND IT'S HEAVIER, TOO.

THEY HAVE TO LUG AROUND MORE EQUIPMENT,

HM?

BUT IF I LEARN HOW TO SHOOT ONE, I'LL BE ABLE TO HELP YOU GUYS OUT, WON'T I?

YOU DON'T NEED TO PRACTICE USING GUNS, ARATA.

IF YOU'RE BORED, JUST TAKE A NAP OR SOMETHING!

DASH

YOU CAN'T!

SWIPE

.....

BA SHAM

SORRY ABOUT EARLIER.

O-OH, IT'S FINE.

TAKE A NAP, HUH?

UMM...

MOST MERCENARY GROUPS DON'T REALLY USE PISTOLS. THEY'RE GOOD FOR INDOOR FIGHTS OR CERTAIN SPECIAL OPS, BUT OTHERWISE RIFLES ARE BETTER.

WHAT DO YOU MEAN, RARE?

YEAH, I WAS KINDA SURPRISED TO SEE SOMETHING SO RARE...

DID YOU SEE THE PISTOL?

YEAH, I THOUGHT CHINA MOSTLY MANUFACTURED RUSSIAN MODELS.

WELL, I IMAGINE YOU'RE SURPRISED WE ALL USE CLONE MODELS MADE BY THE CHINESE GOVERNMENT.

PISTOLS HAVE TOO SHORT A RANGE TO BE USEFUL FOR THOSE.

I SEE...

AND 80% OF OUR JOBS SO FAR HAVE BEEN ESCORT MISSIONS.

REALLY?

WHY'S THAT?

ON TOP OF THAT, .45 CALIBER PISTOLS HAVE BECOME MORE POPULAR IN THE INTERNATIONAL MARKET LATELY.

THE REASON SO MANY OF THEM ARE FLOATING AROUND IS BECAUSE THE M1911'S PATENT EXPIRED.

THEY NEED LARGE-CALIBER PISTOLS TO ACTUALLY DO ANY DAMAGE.

ALL THE CRIME GANGS HAVE TOP-OF-THE-LINE KEVLAR VESTS, SO WHEN WARS BETWEEN RIVAL GANGS BREAK OUT,

FOR THE SAME REASON, LAW ENFORCEMENT AGENCIES CAN'T MAKE DO WITH 10MM BULLETS ANYMORE.

BODY ARMOR IS NOW.

BECAUSE OF HOW MUCH MORE ADVANCED

NOT REALLY.

ARE YOU INTERESTED IN PISTOLS?

.....

THAT MAKES SENSE.

I SEE.

AH...

I FIGURED AS MUCH.

I DON'T WANT TO TURN MY KIDS INTO CRIMINALS,

AND I'D PREFER TO AVOID ASSOCIATING WITH CRIMINALS AS MUCH AS POSSIBLE.

WHY IS IT

SURE.

BY THE WAY, CAN I ASK YOU SOMETHING? I'VE BEEN WONDERING ABOUT THIS SINCE I FIRST MET YOU.

THAT YOU USE KIDS INSTEAD OF ADULTS?

AHAHA-HAHA.

• • • • •

I COULD HAVE JUST LEFT THEM TO KILL EACH OTHER AND GONE HOME.

IF I'D BEEN IN CHARGE OF ADULTS, I PROBABLY WOULDN'T HAVE BOTHERED TAKING CARE OF THEM.

I DON'T THINK I WOULD HAVE BOTHERED TO GET INVOLVED IN THIS BUSINESS AT ALL.

BUT...

43

I COULDN'T BRING MYSELF TO TELL THEM

SO I DIDN'T HAVE A CHOICE.

IT TURNED OUT THE SOLDIERS I WORKED WITH AT MY OLD COMPANY WERE ALL CHILD SOLDIERS,

"GO KILL EACH OTHER FOR ALL I CARE."

IT'S NOT YOU I'M MAD AT, ITOU-SAN.

YOU'RE ANGRY, AREN'T YOU?

UM...

I UNDERSTAND.

LEAN

. . . .

AREN'T YOU A BIT TOO CLOSE?

I KNOW. I'M DOING IT ON PURPOSE.

THIS IS THE FIRST TIME SOMEONE'S ADMITTED THEY'RE TRYING TO TRAP ME. I HAVE TO ADMIT, IT'S A NOVEL EXPERIENCE.

DO YOU WANT TO SEE WHAT IT'S LIKE FALLING INTO A HONEY TRAP?

HEY.

YES...

なで…
RUB

なで…
RUB

TREMBLE
プル

プル
TREMBLE

DO YOU KNOW WHAT HONEY TRAPPING IS?

RAISE
スッ

YES.

IS THAT SO?

I PROMISE TO KEEP MY END OF THE BARGAIN, SO YOU DON'T HAVE TO TRY SO HARD TO SEDUCE ME.

UMM, IT LOOKS LIKE YOU'RE EMULATING A BUNCH OF DIFFERENT PERSONALITY TYPES TO CATCH MY INTEREST, BUT YOU DON'T NEED TO WORRY.

STOP!
...

SORRY, I'M NOT USED TO DOING THIS KIND OF THING...

STAND

UMM...

SLAM!

UHH, YOU'RE THE ONE TELLING ME IT'S A TRAP. WHY WOULD I WANT TO?

TURN

ARE YOU SURE YOU DON'T WANT TO GET HONEY TRAPPED?

46

SO WE CAN'T REALLY COMPLAIN.

THEY'RE SMUGGLED GOODS,

IT'S A SHAME THEY'RE ALL OLD GUNS.

YEAH, THAT'S STILL PREFERABLE TO A GUN WITH AN OVERLY COMPLEX SAFETY SYSTEM. THOSE TAKE TOO LONG TO DISENGAGE IN A CRISIS.

IGNORING THE FACT THAT THESE MODELS DON'T HAVE SAFETIES, DO YOU THINK THEY'RE USABLE?

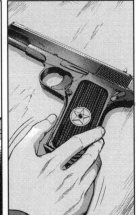

AHH... OUR CLIENT SAID THE SAME THING EARLIER. APPARENTLY EVEN CIVILIANS CAN GET THEIR HANDS ON BULLETPROOF VESTS THESE DAYS.

THEY HAVEN'T BEEN ABLE TO KEEP UP WITH ADVANCEMENTS IN PROTECTIVE GEAR.

THOUGH, RUSSIAN GUNS AREN'T VERY POPULAR THESE DAYS, WITH THE EXCEPTION OF A FEW TOKAREV MODELS... EITHER WAY, THEY'RE NOT GONNA BE OF ANY USE FOR OUR CURRENT MISSION.

WHY AREN'T THEY POPULAR?

BUT BECAUSE GUNS HAVE BECOME SUCH A PROBLEM IN MODERN SOCIETY, A LOT OF GOVERNMENTS HAVE BEEN SLAPPING RESTRICTIONS ON MANUFACTURERS, MAKING IT IMPOSSIBLE FOR THEM TO MAKE AND SELL THE LATEST MILITARY-GRADE GUNS TO THE PUBLIC.

SO THAT'S WHY THEY'RE REVAMPING OLD LARGE-CALIBER MODELS FOR MODERN USE?

YEAH, SO CIVILIAN GUN MANUFACTURERS HAVE HAD TO MODIFY THEIR DESIGNS AS A RESULT.

I SEE...

THE COLT GOVERNMENT WAS ALWAYS POPULAR IN AMERICA, SO IT'S NOT SURPRISING EVERYONE STARTED USING IT ONCE THE PATENT EXPIRED.

BANG

THE BEST PART IS THESE USE THE SAME BULLETS AS THE SUBMACHINE GUNS WE GOT.

THE MAUSER'S ALWAYS BEEN POPULAR IN CHINA. THEY'VE BEEN PRODUCING THEM SINCE BEFORE WWII.

THEY USE THE SAME TYPE OF AMMO.

BY THE WAY, I NOTICED THERE'S MAUSERS AND TOKAREVS HERE TOO...

GRIN

THERE'S A BUNCH OF EXTRA STOCK LEFT FROM THOSE DAYS, SO THEY'VE BEEN GETTING REFURBISHED AND RESOLD.

THAT'S REASSURING.

OHHH!

カチッ
CLICK

SO THESE CAN BE A SUBSTITUTE FOR ASSAULT RIFLES...

WE'LL PROBABLY WANT TO MAKE A MAUSER AND SUBMACHINE GUN THE STANDARD LOADOUT FOR THIS OPERATION.

AND FOR CLOSE-RANGE FIGHTS, WE'VE GOT THE SUBMACHINE GUNS.

WE'RE SHORT ON ASSAULT RIFLES, BUT THE MAUSERS SHOULD BE ABLE TO MAKE UP FOR THAT.

スチャ
SNAP

YEAH, AS LONG AS YOU USE 'EM LIKE THIS.

I SEE... IF YOU USE BOTH HANDS, YOU CAN SOFTEN THE RECOIL.

STILL, IT'S WEIRD TO THINK WE'RE ABOUT TO HAVE A SHOOT OUT USING 100-YEAR OLD GUNS.

BANG!

TREMBLE

TREMBLE

GRAB

HUMANS REALLY ARE FOOLISH CREATURES.

IN PRETENDING TO BE WISE, WE BECOME YET MORE FOOLISH.

THAT'S A SOCRATES QUOTE,

ISN'T IT?

Huh?

EVERYONE IN MY VILLAGE REALLY LIKED SOCRATES.

I RECOGNIZE THAT NAME, BUT I DIDN'T REALIZE IT WAS HIS QUOTE. YOU SURE KNOW A LOT, HAKIM.

WHAT THE...

ブ

ROLL

ニコ GRIN

ALL OF YOU GET IN LINE.

FINE, FINE.

STAND
サッ

THE REAL FOOL HERE IS...

FOOLS, HUH?

OW!

I THINK I TWISTED MY ANKLE.

SHAKE

**HEY, THAT'S NOT FAIR!**

YOU'RE TOO OLD FOR THIS, JINI.

SHAKE

TURN

EVERYONE GET BACK TO TARGET PRACTICE.

AL-RIGHT.

I'M GOING OUT TO BUY EVERYONE LUNCH. I WANT YOU TO COME WITH ME.

JIBRIL.

*What? I'm not that old...*

OKAY.

IT'S FINE...

GUARDING YOU IS MY JOB.

THANKS FOR COMING ALONG.

I BET EVERYONE'S STARVING.

LET'S HURRY BACK.

OKAY.

DOES IT FEEL... NOSTALGIC?

IT'S PRETTY HOT TODAY.

NAH.

BUT IT'S DIFFERENT FROM THE KIND OF HEAT WE GET IN TAJIKISTAN.

.....

YOU DON'T NEED TO!

I FIGURE I SHOULD LEARN ENOUGH TO PROTECT MYSELF AT LEAST.

I... DON'T WANT YOU USING GUNS.

ARATA, YOU WERE TALKING TO THE CAPTAIN ABOUT GUNS EARLIER, WEREN'T YOU?

YOU CAN READ MAPS, AND YOU KNOW ABOUT A LOT OF STUFF.

YOU'RE GOOD AT EVERYTHING YOU DO, ARATA.

YOU JUST DON'T NEED TO DO ANY MORE.

YOU KNOW HOW TO NAVIGATE FOREIGN COUNTRIES.

DO I REALLY LOOK THAT CLUMSY TO YOU? I'M NO EXPERT, BUT I'M SURE—

IT'S NOT THAT YOU'RE CLUMSY.

HUH?

AND YOU LIKE MAIDS.

YOU CAN EVEN EAT THOSE STRANGE FRIED FUNGI CLUMPS WITHOUT A PROBLEM.

FOR STARTERS, STOP CALLING MUSHROOMS FUNGI CLUMPS. THEY'RE NORMAL FOOD, OKAY?

U-UM...

YOU FLEW IN FROM SOMEWHERE FAR AWAY, AND YOU CAN SEE OUR ENEMIES' MOVEMENTS LIKE YOU'RE WATCHING THEM FROM ABOVE.

IT'S LIKE THERE ARE REALLY WINGS GROWING OUT OF YOUR BACK.

WHAT DOES ANY OF THAT HAVE TO DO WITH WHY I SHOULDN'T LEARN HOW TO USE GUNS?

THERE'S A LOT I WANT TO SAY ABOUT THE REST OF YOUR SPEECH TOO, BUT...

YOU WON'T NEED US ANY-MORE.

I'M WORRIED THAT...

BECAUSE IF YOU LEARN HOW TO USE GUNS...

THAT WILL

NEVER HAPPEN!

SORRY.

JUST BECAUSE I VALUE YOUR SHOOTING SKILLS, PLEASE DON'T THINK THAT'S ALL I CARE ABOUT...

I'M NOT KEEPING YOU GUYS AROUND

IT'S NOT OUR CIRCUM-STANCES I HATE,

BUT MY OWN POWER-LESS-NESS.

DON'T WORRY.

NO MATTER WHAT HAPPENS, I WON'T LEAVE YOUR SIDE.

BUT NOW... I'M THE ONE TAKING YOU TO THE BATTLE-FIELD.

WHEN I FIRST SAW THAT YOU KIDS WERE BEING FORCED TO FIGHT,

I THOUGHT IT WAS WRONG.

I CONSIDER MYSELF FORTUNATE TO BE IN THIS SITUATION.

IF ANY-THING...

THE TRULY FOOLISH ONE HERE

IS ME.

OH...

WHAT HAPPENED TO ITOU-SAN?

FEEL FREE.

UHH, IS IT ALRIGHT IF I EAT MY LUNCH?

.....

WHO KNOWS.

WHETHER OR NOT IT'S ALSO UNFORTUNATE FOR US DEPENDS ON THE DETAILS.

WHAT HAPPENED?

スッ
SIT

SOME RATHER UNFORTUNATE NEWS.

WE JUST RECEIVED

I BELIEVE WE DID A THOROUGH JOB ERASING ANY EVIDENCE THAT COULD LINK US TO THE ATTACK.

FIRST OF ALL, WE'VE DISCOVERED THAT THE ARMED CULT WE WANT YOU TO ELIMINATE WAS WORKING TOGETHER WITH THE ASIAN CRIME SYNDICATE YOU ATTACKED.

I'M SORRY, I SHOULD HAVE BEEN MORE SPECIFIC.

AS OF RIGHT NOW, WE CAN'T BE SURE.

DOES THIS MEAN THE PRIORITY OF OUR TARGETS HAS CHANGED?

WAS BETWEEN THE CRIME GANG AND THE CULT.

THE DEAL YOU INTERRUPTED YESTERDAY

WOULD IT BE POSSIBLE FOR YOU TO LEAK INFORMATION TO OUR OPPONENTS?

COULD YOU TELL THEM THAT WE'RE PROTECTING THE CULT'S FOUNDER?

IF WE LEAK THIS, THE CULT WILL BE EXPECTING RESISTANCE AND PREPARE ACCORDINGLY.

THIS OVERSIGHT IS OUR RESPONSIBILITY, SO WE'LL GLADLY COOPERATE.

BUT ARE YOU SURE YOU WANT TO DO THAT?

DEALING WITH TWO DIFFERENT TARGETS AT ONCE IS DIFFICULT.

IN WHICH CASE...

.....

I'M AWARE, BUT...

VERY WELL.

AND COME AT US ALL AT ONCE.

I'D RATHER THE ENEMY COMBINE THEIR FORCES...

WHAT ABOUT ARTILLERY?

CONSIDERING HOW DIFFICULT IT WOULD BE TO IMPORT THOSE, I DOUBT IT, BUT WE BELIEVE THEY HAVE ACCESS TO MACHINE GUNS AND ROCKET LAUNCHERS.

UNLIKELY.

THE CRIME SYNDICATE FEELS AS THOUGH THEIR HONOR HAS BEEN TARNISHED... THEY MAY BRING OUT THE BIG GUNS.

HOW BIG ARE WE TALKING? DO THEY HAVE TANKS AND ASSAULT HELICOPTERS?

IN THAT CASE... WE SHOULD BE ABLE TO MANAGE.

UNDERSTOOD.

IT HAS THE SPECIFICATIONS YOU REQUESTED.

WE'VE MANAGED TO SECURE AN I-ILLUMINATOR FOR YOU.

I'M SORRY. THIS IS OUR FAULT FOR MISREADING THE ENEMY'S MOVEMENTS. I REALIZE THIS WON'T MAKE UP FOR IT, BUT...

THAT'S FINE.

I'M AFRAID IT'S AN AMERICAN MODEL THOUGH, AS OUR DOMESTIC ONES ARE STILL IN TESTING.

AS LONG AS I HAVE ONE, WE CAN OPERATE AT 90% OF OUR OPTIMAL FIGHTING STRENGTH.

NO, YOU'RE THE SPECIALIST. I'LL TRUST YOUR EVALUATION.

I UNDERSTAND YOUR SKEPTICISM, BUT...

IT'S THAT IMPORTANT?

HE'LL DELIVER THE GOODS TO YOU TOMORROW.

THIS IS THE RENDEZVOUS POINT.

YOU'RE ACQUAINTED WITH CLAUD LANSON, CORRECT? THE MANAGER OF THE FAR EAST BRANCH?

HE'S MY OLD BOSS.

REGARDLESS, WE BOUGHT IT FROM THE COMPANY YOU USED TO WORK FOR. WE ALREADY HAVE THE AMERICAN GOVERNMENT'S AUTHORIZATION FOR THE PURCHASE, SO YOU DON'T NEED TO WORRY ABOUT THAT.

PLEASE MOVE HIM SOMEWHERE SUITABLE FOR A FIREFIGHT. PREFERABLY SOMEWHERE HE WOULD NATURALLY RESIDE.

WE'VE TAKEN HIM TO A SAFE HOUSE.

INCIDENTALLY, WHERE IS THE CULT LEADER RIGHT NOW?

WOULD YOU BE ABLE TO GET SOME MORE FOR US?

BY THE WAY, WE'RE A LITTLE SHORT ON BULLETS...

I'LL SEE WHAT I CAN DO.

HOW QUICKLY CAN HE BE RELOCATED?

WORKS FOR ME.

I REALIZE THAT WAS ORIGINALLY OUR OPPONENT'S BASE OF OPERATIONS, BUT... WHAT DO YOU THINK OF MOVING HIM THERE?

DO YOU REMEMBER THE TRAINING FACILITY IN GUNMA WE TOLD YOU ABOUT?

IT'LL TAKE A DAY.

.....

I CAN TEST THE I-ILLUMINATOR AND FORMULATE A PLAN ON-SITE.

I CAN CALIBRATE IT ON MY WAY TO GUNMA AND MEET UP WITH OMAR AND THE OTHERS THERE.

I'LL BE GETTING MY I-ILLUMINATOR TOMORROW MORNING.

CONSIDERING HOW LONG IT'LL TAKE, IT'S BEST TO MOVE HIM RIGHT AWAY.

MEANING IT'LL BE TOMORROW NIGHT AT THE EARLIEST BEFORE WE'RE READY TO FIGHT.

BUT ARE YOU SURE YOU WANT TO MOVE THIS FAST? WE'RE NOT UNDER ANY TIME CONSTRAINTS.

WILL DO.

BUT DON'T LEAK THE INTEL TO OUR ENEMY UNTIL THREE DAYS FROM NOW.

UNDERSTOOD. HAVE THE CULT LEADER MOVED RIGHT AWAY.

EXCUSE ME. I NEED TO PREPARE.

RIGHT NOW, I HAVE NO WAY OF PREDICTING HOW THEY'LL MOVE.

AND THAT'S THE MOST DANGEROUS SITUATION TO BE IN.

ズッ
STAND

I WANT TO NARROW DOWN THE ENEMY'S POTENTIAL COURSES OF ACTION AS SOON AS POSSIBLE.

GOTCHA, I'LL SPEED UP OUR PREPARATIONS THEN.

I CAN'T TELL IF THEY'RE PLANNING ON GOING STRAIGHT AFTER THE CULT LEADER, OR TRYING TO TAKE US OUT FIRST.

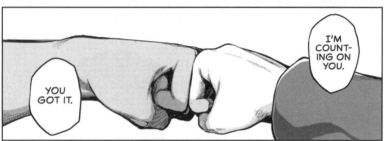

YOU GOT IT.

I'M COUNTING ON YOU.

I'M GOING BACK TO TOKYO, DO YOU FEEL LIKE BEING MY BODY-GUARD AGAIN?

*JIBRIL!*

YES, SIR!

PLEASE LET ME COME WITH YOU!

SURE.

COME ON, FOLLOW ME.

## OPERATION_026
# REUNION AT THE PARK

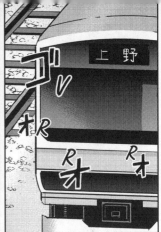

上野

ゴ

HMM, WHERE SHOULD I START...

SO, WHAT'S GOING ON?

OH YEAH...

I GUESS I DID.

YOU SAID YOU'D TELL ME YOUR COMPLAINTS FROM NOW ON.

THE TWO GROUPS HAVE JOINED FORCES.

ACCORDING TO WHAT OUR CLIENT HAS SAID,

AND THEY WERE IN THE MIDDLE OF A DEAL WITH OUR PRIMARY TARGET WHEN WE ATTACKED THEM.

WELL, THE PEOPLE WE STOLE WEAPONS FROM YESTERDAY ARE A LARGE-SCALE CHINESE-BASED CRIME SYNDICATE,

**ム**ッ
*FROWN*

I THINK THEY'RE TESTING US.

THEY WANT TO KNOW WHETHER WE'LL SERVE JAPAN'S INTERESTS OR NOT.

WHY IS OUR CLIENT BARELY TELLING US ANYTHING THIS TIME?

WE'RE MERCENARIES. IT'S OUR JOB TO SELL OUR CAPACITY FOR VIOLENCE

TO THE HIGHEST BIDDER.

THAT BEING SAID, IT'S NOT LIKE ANYTHING ABOUT OUR JOB WOULD HAVE CHANGED IF WE KNEW ALL THAT FROM THE START.

OR AT THE VERY LEAST,

IS ELIMINATE THE ENEMY.

RENDER THEM POWERLESS.

WHAT THEY REALLY WANT US TO DO...

OUR CLIENT SAID THIS WOULD BE AN ESCORT MISSION, BUT THAT WAS JUST AN EXCUSE TO HIRE US.

SORRY.

YOU DON'T HAVE TO LOOK SO ANNOYED.

ANYWAY...

.....

71

I SEE.

SO WHERE IN TOKYO ARE WE GOING?

TO MAKE MATTERS WORSE, I HAVE NO IDEA HOW EFFECTIVE THEIR INTELLIGENCE NETWORK IS.

REGARDLESS, THIS PUTS US IN A TIGHT SPOT.

THE PROBLEM IS OUR ADVERSARY, AND THE ORGANIZATION THEY'VE JOINED FORCES WITH, FEEL LIKE WE'VE TARNISHED THEIR REPUTATION. MEANING IT'S HIGHLY LIKELY THEY'LL TARGET US NOW.

THERE...

THEN TOMORROW MORNING WE NEED TO GO TO SHINJUKU CENTRAL PARK.

WE'LL SPEND THE NIGHT AT UENO.

AFTER THAT,

WE'LL MEET UP WITH EVERYONE ELSE.

I'LL PICK UP MY I-ILLUMINATOR.

THE RECENT INCIDENT LEFT EVERYONE RATTLED.

I DO, BUT I GOT THE DAY OFF.

YO.

DON'T YOU WORK NEAR KAWAWSAKI? PRETTY SURE I SAW YOU AT ONE OF THE PARKS THERE.

ニコ・・・
GRIN

I SEE...

BY THE WAY, BROTHER...

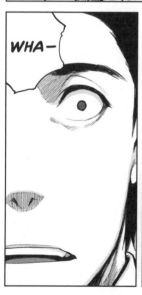

WHA—

PUBLIC PARKS AREN'T REALLY SUITED FOR THAT KINDA THING.

POINT
ピッ

IF YOU'RE LOOKING FOR A LOVE HOTEL, I'D SAY CHECK OUT KABUKI-CHOU.

IF YOU TRY TO SUPPRESS YOUR WORLDLY DESIRES, THEY'LL JUST GET IN YOUR WAY AT THE WORST POSSIBLE MOMENT.

BUT IF YOU INDULGE THEM, YOU'LL BE ABLE TO CLEAR YOUR MIND AND REACH NIRVANA AFTERWARDS.

MIGHT AS WELL GET IT ON NOW BEFORE THINGS GET BUSY.

ALL I'M SAYING IS YOU SHOULD SOW YOUR SEED WHILE THE TIME IS RIPE.

EXCUSE ME?

EXCUSE ME, I'M IN A HURRY.

UH-HUH.

TURN
ス"

THE BALD GUY WITH NO EYEBROWS AND A BEARD IS AN ENFORCER.

AND THE OTHER MAN HAS MILITARY TRAINING.

NOT REALLY... WE'VE ONLY TALKED ONCE.

WAS THAT SOME-ONE YOU KNOW?

IT DIDN'T LOOK LIKE EITHER OF THEM WERE CARRYING GUNS...

HUH?

AND PEOPLE WHO'VE SPENT A LONG TIME HOLDING ASSAULT RIFLES CARRY THEM-SELVES A CERTAIN WAY.

THERE'S ONLY A FEW PLACES ON YOUR BODY WHERE YOU CAN HIDE A PISTOL, SO IT'S EASY TO TELL IF YOU KNOW WHERE TO LOOK.

I GUESS THERE'S GUYS LIKE THAT, EVEN IN JAPAN.

THOUGH THERE'S PROBABLY LESS HERE THAN IN OTHER COUNTRIES.

I SEE...

IT FEELS NICE TO TEACH YOU SOMETHING FOR ONCE, ARATA!

ふん HEH

HEH ふん

TWITCH

SO...

WHAT DID HE TALK TO YOU ABOUT?

WE, UH...

WELL...

UMM...

JUST DISCUSSED THE WEATHER.

BOW
ズッ

LONG
TIME
NO
SEE.

I HAD A
FEELING
WE'D
MEET
AGAIN.

YOU
MADE
IT.

OUR ELF THOUGHT YOU WERE DEAD, BUT...

I KNEW YOU WOULDN'T KICK THE BUCKET THAT EASILY.

JIBRIL.

KEEP AN EYE ON OUR SURROUNDINGS.

I DIDN'T EXPECT TO SEE YOU AGAIN HERE IN TOKYO OF ALL PLACES.

WELL, MY SAVIOR WAS JAPANESE, SO I FIGURED I SHOULD AT LEAST PAY MY RESPECTS.

IT'S A BIT LATE, BUT I'VE FINALLY DELIVERED MY REPORT.

ALL THE SOLDIERS THAT WERE WITH ME THAT NIGHT ARE STILL ALIVE.

OH YEAH...

.....

NOT ONLY DID YOU SAVE OUR LIVES, YOU SAVED A PLATOON TRAPPED IN ENEMY TERRITORY.

YOU REALLY ARE SOMETHING ELSE.

SO THAT'S WHAT HAPPENED.

I SEE...

YOU KNOW,

IT'S KINDA NOSTALGIC

BEING PRAISED BY MY OLD BOSS.

THE MERC PEOPLE CALL THE "HEADMASTER," ALSO KNOWN AS THE GOLDEN EAGLE...

SO, TELL ME...

THAT'S YOU, ISN'T IT?

80

OUR ELF'LL BE BRINGING IT TO YOU. SHE SHOULD BE HERE SOON.

ABOUT THE I-ILLU-MINATOR YOU ORDERED.

THANK YOU VERY MUCH.

AH, SORRY. NOW'S NOT THE TIME TO BE CATCHING UP.

.....

I'D LIKE TO ASK FOR YOUR ADVICE ON SOME-THING.

UMM... BY THE WAY...

WELL, I'M NOT SURE THERE'S ANY-THING LEFT FOR ME TO TEACH YOU.

BUT IF YOU WANT MY ADVICE, I'D BE HAPPY TO GIVE IT.

AND NOW...

THERE'S SO MUCH I'VE SEEN AND DONE.

WELL...

EVER SINCE JOINING THE FREEDOM FIGHTERS,

WHERE EVERYONE'S CALLING ME THE HEADMASTER.

I'M STUCK IN THIS SITUATION

BUT YOU KNOW, DESPITE WHAT EVERYONE MIGHT THINK,

I'M DESPERATE.

.....

I WANT TO BE ABLE TO GIVE THESE KIDS A FUTURE WHERE THEY DON'T HAVE TO WIELD GUNS.

THAT'S WHAT I'VE BEEN FIGHTING SO FRANTICALLY FOR.

LOOM

I DON'T KNOW IF I'M DOING THE RIGHT THING ANYMORE.

BUT...

.....

GRIP

SO... YOU'RE WONDERING HOW YOU SHOULD PROCEED FROM HERE?

YES...

I KEEP TELLING MYSELF "SOMEDAY, SOMEDAY," BUT...

WHEN IT COMES DOWN TO IT, I HAVE TO KEEP SENDING THOSE 24 KIDS OUT ON THE BATTLEFIELD JUST TO PUT FOOD ON THE TABLE.

SORRY.

THAT'S QUITE THE DIFFICULT DILEMMA YOU'RE GRAPPLING WITH.

HAHA-HAHA.

?

WHEN I WAS STATIONED IN CENTRAL ASIA, THERE WAS A TIME I NEARLY LOST MY LIFE.

. . . . .

THAT WAS ONE HELL OF A NIGHT.

EVEN NOW, IT FEELS LIKE IT WAS ALL A DREAM.

84

JUST WHEN I'D GIVEN UP ALL HOPE, ONE OF MY SUBORDINATES, WHO I BELIEVED HAD BEEN TAKEN CAPTIVE,

MANAGED, WITH A SINGLE WIRELESS TRANCEIVER,

TO CHANGE EVERYTHING.

ALL WHILE BEING DOZENS OF MILES AWAY.

EVEN THOUGH HE HAD NO WAY OF SEEING OUR CURRENT SITUATION,

HE SAVED OUR LIVES.

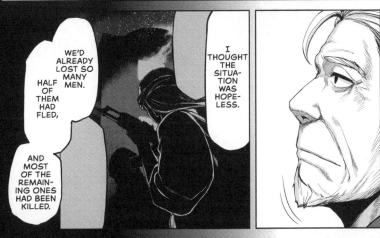

HALF OF THEM HAD FLED,

WE'D ALREADY LOST SO MANY MEN.

AND MOST OF THE REMAINING ONES HAD BEEN KILLED.

I THOUGHT THE SITUATION WAS HOPELESS.

YOU'RE THE SAME

AS WHEN I FIRST MET YOU.

YOU REALLY HAVEN'T CHANGED AT ALL, HUH.

YOU HAVE THE POWER

TO MOLD REALITY ACCORDING TO YOUR WISHES.

IT'S FINE TO BE LOST.

BUT NO MATTER WHAT,

DON'T STOP STRUGGLING.

THUD
コツ...

I'M AFRAID THAT'S ALL THE ADVICE I CAN GIVE YOU.

PERSONALLY, I THINK YOU'RE FINE THE WAY YOU ARE.

FWOOSH.

THUD

NGH...

SHIT!

MY VISION'S ALL BLURRY!

WHAT JUST HAP-PENED?

ARE WE UNDER ATTACK?

CAN YOU STAND, JIBRIL!?

YES!

BUT...

I'M NOT SURE.

ゴ U オ M オ M ブ し オ E

WHATEVER THIS IS...

SOMEONE'S BLOWN UP THE BRIDGE. THE FAR SIDE'S STILL ON FIRE.

OUR ONLY OPTION IS TO RETREAT TOWARD THE WATERFALL.

ARE YOU OKAY!?

WE CAN'T GO THAT WAY.

NO...

THIS IS A TRAP.

WHY NOT?

THERE HAS TO BE A REASON WHY WHO-EVER DID THIS SET FIRE TO THE SURROUNDINGS AS WELL AS BLOW UP THE BRIDGE.

THE ONLY SUITABLE LOCATION FOR A SNIPER TO SET UP WITHIN THIS PARK IS THE AREA WE'RE IN RIGHT NOW.

AN EXPLOSION OF THAT SIZE WOULDN'T CREATE FLAMES THIS LARGE.

WAIT!

EVERYONE'S RUNNING TOWARD THE WATERFALL!

IF THESE ASSAILANTS WERE WARY OF BEING SNIPED, THEY'D USE THE EXPLOSIONS AND THE FLAMES TO DRAW PEOPLE AWAY.

Waterfall

Elevated Ground

Fire

MOREOVER, THEY'D USE THE SUBSEQUENT EXPLOSIONS TO LIMIT PEOPLE'S PATH OF RETREAT, LEADING THEM DOWN THE ROUTE THEY WANT.

NOT YET.

DO YOU SEE ANY SIGN OF THE ENEMY?

JIBRIL!

THEY PROBABLY DON'T HAVE A LOT OF TROOPS.

I SEE...

WHICH IS WHY THEY'RE RESORTING TO CLEVER TRICKS LIKE THIS.

IS THERE

WE HAVE NO WEAPONS...

ANYTHING WE CAN USE?

LET ME SEE THOSE BINOCULARS.

GRIP
スッ

RIP

TEAR

RIP

DO YOU...

THE SCREAMS ARE MAKING IT HARD TO CONCEN-TRATE.

DAM-MIT!

# M.O.05

MARGINAL OPERATION

## OPERATION_027
# THE ELF'S BOW

CLICK

•••••

IF WE HAVE NO WEAP-ONS...

HOW CAN WE PROCEED...

OMAR SPEAKING. WHAT'S UP?

NO CHOICE BUT TO TRY.

Omar

BEEP

IF NOT, WHAT ABOUT THAT OLD LADY?

IS ITOU-SAN, OUR CLIENT, OVER THERE!?

I DON'T SEE EITHER OF THEM...

SORRY, BUT THIS IS AN EMERGENCY. I'LL CALL YOU BACK LATER!

GOOD.

Unknown

BEEP

!!!

WHY? DID SOMETHING HA—

WE'RE AWARE OF THE SITUATION.

IS THAT YOU, ITOU-SAN? THANK GOD YOU GUYS WERE MONITORING MY CALLS.

THEN I'LL MAKE THIS QUICK. I'M ON THE SCENE.

104

I'M AFRAID THE MILITARY ISN'T UNDER MY JURIS-DICTION, SO I CAN'T GIVE THEM ORDERS.

HOWEVER... I WILL TRY AND ASK.

IF YOU DON'T HURRY, MORE CIVILIANS ARE GOING TO DIE.

SEND A SNIPER OVER TO MY LOCATION ASAP.

I'LL HAVE TO CONTACT THE FIRE DEPARTMENT AS WELL THEN... UNFORTUNATELY, THEY'RE NOT UNDER MY JURISDICTION EITHER, SO IT'LL TAKE SOME TIME.

ALL THIS RED TAPE...

THE ROAD LEADING TO OUR LOCATION IS BLOCKED BY FIRE.

.....

HOW LONG WILL IT TAKE TO GET SOME-ONE HERE!?

I'M SORRY, BUT 30 MINUTES IS THE BEST I CAN DO.

THE LIVES OF YOUR CITIZENS ARE DE-PENDING ON YOU!

PLEASE HURRY!

TAP

BUT...

THE NEXT HALF HOUR IS GOING TO BE HELL.

WHAT DO THESE GUYS—

30 MINUTES, HUH?

WE ARE THE CIRCLE OF ENLIGHTENMENT!

AND WE HAVE RISEN UP TO SHOW THE WORLD THE TRUE PATH OF BUDDHISM!

HOWEVER, IN ORDER TO PUSH BACK THE DARKNESS, THE HEARTS OF PEOPLE MUST BECOME ONE. IT IS ONLY THE MERCY OF MAN THAT CAN CALL DOWN THE LIGHT FROM HEAVEN!

OUR LEADER, THE ILLUSTRIOUS NICHIRIN KOUSUTAI HAS TAUGHT US THAT ONLY THE LIGHT FROM THE HEAVENS CAN TRULY CLEANSE THIS EVIL!

LIGHT ALWAYS CASTS A SHADOW, BUT THE GOODNESS IN PEOPLE'S HEARTS CAN SERVE AS A BEACON!

THE LIGHT OF ENLIGHTENMENT ONLY FOR THOSE WHO FOLLOW THE CORRECT TEACHINGS! WE ARE HERE TO SAVE THE WORLD!

FOR HE ON HIGH IS OUR GUIDING LIGHT!

HIS ASCENSION TO ENLIGHTENMENT IS PROOF THAT THE GREAT BUDDHA BELIEVES SALVATION CAN ONLY COME THROUGH OUR SELFLESS OFFERING!

NICHIRIN KOUSHOUTAI... HE'S THE MAN WE'RE SUPPOSED TO BE PROTECTING. BUT I STILL DON'T UNDERSTAND WHAT THESE GUYS ARE AFTER.

THEY'RE SPOUTING ALL THIS CRAP ABOUT TRUE BUDDHISM, BUT WHAT THEY'RE DOING ISN'T BUDDHIST IN THE LEAST.

!!

IT'S ONLY BEEN FIVE MINUTES.

DO WE REALLY HAVE TO WAIT HERE FOR ANOTHER 25?

WHAT THE?

SOPHIE!

CLACK

STEP

RUMBLE

RUSTLE

LANSON TOLD ME TO WAIT UNTIL HE GAVE FURTHER ORDERS...

BUT WHEN THE FIRE BROKE OUT...

WHAT ARE YOU DOING HERE!?

SLIDE

OH...

I KNEW YOU WERE HERE, ARATA,

SO I HAD TO COME SAVE YOU.

YOU BROUGHT YOUR CROSS-BOW WITH YOU, RIGHT?

YES.

IT'S STILL IN THE CAR.

BUT IT'S TOO LATE TO GO BACK FOR IT NOW...

WHAT ABOUT THE I-ILLU-MINA-TOR?

110

BUT IT'S GOING TO BE IMPOSSIBLE TO TAKE ON A GROUP ARMED WITH ASSAULT RIFLES

WITH JUST ONE CROSSBOW.

DON'T WORRY, I'LL ORDER ANOTHER ONE FOR YOU.

THANKS, I APPRECIATE IT.

THAT'S NOT TRUE.

NO...

GOT ONE RIGHT HERE.

THOUGH, WE'LL NEED A MIRROR...

I HAVE ONE TOO.

CONSIDERING THE SITUATION, AS LONG AS THE CROSSBOW'S CAPABLE OF SNIPING A GOOD DISTANCE AWAY, WE CAN DO THIS.

IN THAT CASE,

FWIP

GRIN

I'VE GOT YOU COVERED!

HOW ACCURATE DO YOU NEED THE CROSSBOW TO BE?

AS LONG AS YOU CAN HIT SOMEONE FROM 100 METERS AWAY, THAT SHOULD SUFFICE.

HUH?

EVER SINCE COMING TO JAPAN, SHE'S BEEN PRACTICING WITH CROSSBOWS.

SHE'S TELLING THE TRUTH.

I THOUGHT THEY WERE MORE ELF-LIKE THAN GUNS.

BUT WHY?

**TUG**

**TUG**

COME WITH ME.

I NEED TO FIND OUT IF YOU CAN HIT THESE GUYS OR NOT.

WHAT'S THAT SUP—

**GRAB**

THAT'S SO LIKE YOU. I'M GLAD YOU HAVEN'T CHANGED.

*HAHA HAHA!*

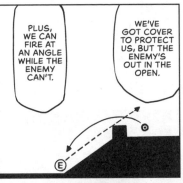

WE'VE GOT COVER TO PROTECT US, BUT THE ENEMY'S OUT IN THE OPEN.

PLUS, WE CAN FIRE AT AN ANGLE WHILE THE ENEMY CAN'T.

YOU'RE GOING TO HAVE TO KEEP YOUR HEAD DOWN AND USE THE MIRROR AS A PERISCOPE TO ADJUST YOUR AIM.

OVER HERE.

THAT IS...

ASSUMING YOU CAN SHOOT ACCURATE-LY FROM HERE...

NOD
コク

WE'LL BE ABLE TO

SLICE

ONE-SIDEDLY PRESSURE THE ENEMY.

ALRIGHT, GET IN SNIPING POSITION.

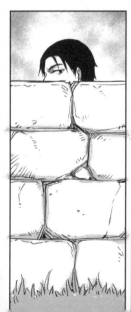

IF THEY START USING THE HOSTAGES AS SHIELDS, STOP FIRING AND RELOCATE.

SOPHIE, IT'S FINE IF YOU MISS, BUT MAKE SURE YOU DON'T HIT THE HOSTAGES.

コク
NOD

I'LL GO TOO.

スッ
FWISH

KEEP YOUR BATON READY AND LIE IN AMBUSH NEAR THE TOP OF THE STAIRS. I'LL INFORM YOU IF ANY-ONE STARTS CLIMBING THEM.

サッ
DASH

JIBRIL, THERE'S A POSSIBILITY THE ENEMY WILL TRY TO RUSH OUR POSITION.

I'M REALLY HAPPY...

I GOT TO SEE YOU AGAIN.

HEY ARATA...

SOPHIE, YOU CAN FIRE WHEN-EVER YOU'RE READY.

TRY TO HIDE,

OR COME AFTER US?

NOW THEN, WILL YOU USE THE HOSTAGES AS SHIELDS,

LOOKS LIKE YOU'RE NOT SURE.

THWACK

ONE ENEMY REMAINING.

ゴトッ

SLUMP

!!!

THWACK

バァ

TREMBLE

バァ

TREMBLE

バァ

TREMBLE

TA

TA

RA

TA

TA

TA

RA

ATA

ATA

TA

RA

TA

ATA

ATA

CRA

CK

JUMP

SL

AM

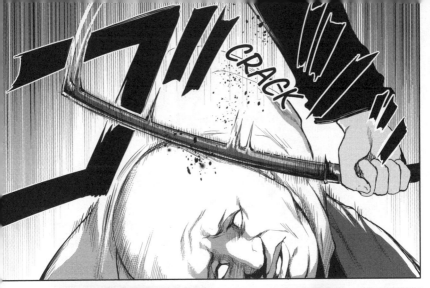

CRACK

.....

ALL
ENEMIES
ELIMI-
NATED.

・・・・・

・・・・・

ブルッ・・・

TREMBLE

WHOA, REALLY? THAT'S SCARY, MAN. LET'S HEAD HOME BEFORE IT GETS DARK.

APPARENTLY IT WAS A CULT-LED TERRORIST ATTACK.

ALRIGHT, WE'LL TALK LATER.

I SEE... YES, THAT'S FINE. I DON'T MIND.

......

SEEMS LIKE OUR OLD COMPANY

IS WILLING TO DEAL WITH WHATEVER INVESTIGA-TION COMES OUT OF THIS IF IT MEANS THEY CAN IN-CREASE THEIR REPUTATION.

OUR CLIENT'S GOING TO GIVE CREDIT TO FREEDOM FIGHTERS FOR STOP-PING THE ATTACK.

!!!!

YO.

NOW THEN, LET'S GO BACK AND SEE WHAT OUR CLIENT—

SO IN THE END...

YOU DIDN'T GO TO KABUKI-CHOU.

.....

YOU KNOW...

THE GUYS BEHIND THAT ATTACK

NOPE.

ARE YOU A FORMER JSDF SOLDIER OR SOMETHING?

I SEE.

REALLY HATED OUR CULT LEADER.

AH... I SEE....

THAT'S NOT WHAT THEY WERE SAYING WHEN THEY WERE GUNNING DOWN INNOCENT PEOPLE.

IT'S AN EFFICIENT PLAN. YOU GET THE BEST RESULTS WHILE LOSING THE FEWEST SOLDIERS.

BUT YOU KNOW...

THEY MADE THE CULT LEADER PUBLIC ENEMY NUMBER ONE.

HE HAD THE MOST RADICAL OF THE CULTISTS STAGE A TERRORIST ATTACK IN THE CULT LEADER'S NAME.

AND BY DOING THAT...

THAT MIGHT BE WHAT IT LOOKS LIKE TO YOU GUYS.

A SUICIDE ATTACK THAT GETS INNOCENT CIVILIANS INVOLVED ISN'T—

THEN THEY REAPED WHAT THEY SOWED.

THAT'S HOW MUCH FAITH THEY HAD IN THE LEADER.

THOSE MEN GAVE UP THEIR WIVES AND DAUGHTERS FOR THE CULT.

BUT THINK OF IT THIS WAY...

128

MONEY,

OR YOUR HOME-LAND...

WHETHER IT BE RELIGION,

EVERYONE BELIEVES IN SOMETHING. WHAT THEY HAPPENED TO BELIEVE IN WAS DIFFERENT THAN MOST PEOPLE, BUT REGARDLESS OF YOUR FAITH, WHEN YOU GET BETRAYED BY THE THING YOU PUT YOUR TRUST IN THE MOST...

COME ON...

DON'T JUDGE THEM SO HARSHLY.

WHO CAN BLAME YOU FOR WANTING TO GIVE OTHERS A TASTE OF THE SUFFERING YOU'VE EXPERIENCED?

WELL...

.....

NEITHER.

MONEY, OR YOUR COUNTRY?

WHICH DO YOU BELIEVE IN?

SO WHAT ABOUT YOU?

LET'S GET OUTTA HERE, KAJITA.

OI!

PAT

I SEE...

THAT WAS SOME GOOD SHOOTING BACK THERE.

SEE YA AROUND, MERCENARY.

IF WE NEVER SAW EACH OTHER AGAIN.

I THINK IT'D BE BEST FOR BOTH OF US...

TAP

TAP

UNFORTUNATELY, WE'RE HONORBOUND TO HELP THEM.

YOU FUCKED UP THOSE GUYS' TURF, AND NOW THEY WANT REVENGE.

THAT'S NOT POSSIBLE.

I'M AFRAID...

YOU'LL ONLY INCREASE THE BODY COUNT.

• • • • •

WE'LL SEE ABOUT THAT.

WELL...

131

AS FAR AS THE GOVERNMENT IS CONCERNED, THE CULT LEADER'S NO LONGER OF ANY VALUE.

THE ENEMY'S PLAN WAS PERFECT.

STEP

STEP

STEP

THEY CAN'T HAVE THAT, SO...

THOUGH, IF THEY DO THAT, HE MIGHT CONFESS TO THINGS THAT ITOU-SAN'S AGENCY WOULDN'T WANT OUT IN THE OPEN.

THEY'LL PROBABLY JUST TURN HIM OVER TO THE POLICE.

GOOD WORK.

THEY'LL PROBABLY...

132

BY THE WAY, THE STORY IS THAT THE POLICE SUBCONTRACTED OUT FREEDOM FIGHTERS FOR A TRIAL PERIOD TO SEE IF THEY'D MAKE THE STREETS SAFER.

THANKS TO YOU, CASUALTIES WERE KEPT TO A MINIMUM.

THAT'S THEIR STORY?

ENOUGH ABOUT THE POLICE. THE CULT LEADER YOU GUYS WERE PROTECTING HAS NO VALUE TO YOU ANYMORE, RIGHT?

OKAY.

OF COURSE, IT'LL BE A BITTER PILL FOR THE POLICE TO SWALLOW, AND THE LOCAL DEPARTMENT HERE WILL PROBABLY BE CONFUSED FOR SOME TIME.

THIS IS THE KIND OF STUFF WE HAVE TO GO WITH WHEN SOMETHING UNPRECEDENTED HAPPENS.

CORRECT.

WHICH IS WHY HE **COMMITTED** SUICIDE.

I TAKE IT THIS MEANS OUR CONTRACT IS CANCELED?

I'M AFRAID SO.

I REGRET THAT THINGS TURNED OUT THIS WAY, AND I DO FEEL LIKE OUR AGENCY IS RESPONSIBLE.

WELL, THAT IS A PROBLEM.

HAAH...

I'M TERRIBLY SORRY THINGS ENDED UP LIKE THIS.

ESPECIALLY AFTER ALL YOUR COOPERATION.

UMM...

WHAT DOES THAT MEAN, CON-CRETE-LY?

.....

UMM...

WHICH IS WHY I'D LIKE TO OFFER WHATEVER ASSISTANCE I CAN.

I'M SURE YOU WANT TO LEAVE THE COUNTRY AS SOON AS POSSIBLE.

I CAN ARRANGE PLANE TICKETS FOR ALL OF YOU.

THAT'S TOO LATE.

HOW SOON CAN YOU HAVE THEM READY?

BY TOMOR-ROW.

WELL...

IF THEY'RE FAST, THEY MIGHT EVEN ATTACK US AS SOON AS TONIGHT.

THE ENEMY'S ALREADY ON THE MOVE.

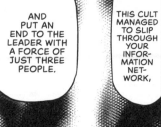

AND PUT AN END TO THE LEADER WITH A FORCE OF JUST THREE PEOPLE.

THIS CULT MANAGED TO SLIP THROUGH YOUR INFORMATION NETWORK,

IN ORDER TO FORESTALL THEM, IT'S IMPERATIVE WE STRIKE FIRST.

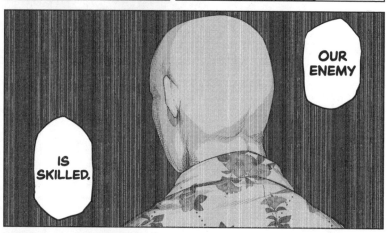

OUR ENEMY

IS SKILLED.

DOES THAT MEAN YOUR ORGANIZATION DOESN'T CARE IF INNOCENTS DIE?

WHEN YOU SAY PERSONALLY...

WHILE I'M PERSONALLY GLAD YOU'RE WORRIED ABOUT OUR CITIZENS, I—

A SHOOT-OUT THERE WOULD LEAD TO MORE CASUALTIES, AND THAT'S SOMETHING I WANT TO AVOID.

EVEN IF THEY DON'T ATTACK TONIGHT, IT'S LIKELY THEY'LL TARGET THE AIRPORT TOMORROW.

ERR...

THAT'S NOT QUITE WHAT I...

WHAT EXACTLY DO YOU WANT?

IF YOUR ORGANIZA-TION'S GOT A PROBLEM WITH THAT TOO, THEN I'M AFRAID YOU'RE GOING TO HAVE TO OFFER MORE SUPPORT.

EITHER FIND A WAY TO GET US OUT OF JAPAN BEFORE TONIGHT, OR MOVE US TO A JSDF OR AMERICAN MILITARY BASE.

IF YOU CAN'T DO EITHER OF THOSE THINGS...

·····

THEN GIVE US PERMISSION

TO STRIKE THE FIRST BLOW.

COULD I... HAVE SOME TIME TO THINK THIS OVER?

BY ALL MEANS.

WELL CONSI-
DERING OUR
SITUATION...

IT'S
PROBABLY
THE BEST
THEY COULD
HAVE DONE.

EXCEPT
WE
DON'T...

ANYWAY,
I HAVE A
MESSAGE
FROM MY
SUPERIORS.

HAHAHA,
WE WERE
JUST
TALKING
ABOUT IT,
ACTUALLY.

THIS
IS ITOU
SPEAKING.
HOW ARE
YOU LIKING
THE BUS?

AS
LONG
AS YOU
LIKE IT.

BEEP
BEEP

Unknown

TAP

THEY'RE FINE WITH YOU BRINGING THE FIGHT TO THE ENEMY, BUT THEY WANT YOU TO KEEP CIVILIAN CASUALTIES TO A MINIMUM,

THAT'S ALL THEY ASK.

UHH... THAT WAS MOSTLY JUST LIP SERVICE. ANYWAY, MAKE SURE YOU HAVE OUR FLIGHT READY FOR TOMORROW.

D-DOES THAT MEAN YOU'RE STILL WILLING TO TAKE ON RE-QUESTS!?

IT'S A SHAME THINGS ENDED UP THE WAY THEY DID THIS TIME AROUND, BUT HOPEFULLY WE CAN HAVE A MORE PRODUC-TIVE RELATION-SHIP IN THE FUTURE.

UNDER-STOOD.

SPARKLE

HUH!?

BYE FOR NOW.

SO I'M SENDING YOU A LIST OF THE CRIME SYNDICATE'S HIDEOUTS. ONCE YOU'VE MEMORIZED THE ADDRES-SES BE SURE TO DELETE IT.

I REALLY DO FEEL BAD ABOUT THIS. IT'S OUR FAULT WE COULDN'T PREDICT THE ENEMY'S MOVEMENTS,

UMM... BY THE WAY...

FINE,

BEEP

POLITICS, HUH...

POLITICS...

WHY DO YOU GUYS LOOK SO DOWN?

.....

NOW LOOK HERE...

IF HE'S BETTER AT FIGHTING, WE JUST HAVE TO MAKE THIS ABOUT WAR INSTEAD OF POLITICS!

OUR GOLDEN EAGLE'S TOO NICE A GUY TO BE GOOD AT POLITICS. HE MIGHT BE A MASTER OF TACTICS, BUT HE'S TERRIBLE AT DECEIVING PEOPLE.

*HAHA HAHA HAHA!*

.....

GOOD POINT.

. . . . .

WHEN IT COMES TO COMBAT...

NO ONE CAN BEAT US.

SCRATCH

SCRATCH

SCRATCH

THEY REALLY ARE A BUNCH OF SORE LOSERS...

WELL, GUESS IT'S NOT A BIG DEAL.

FINALLY, I'LL HAVE ONE AGAIN...

OH, OKAY.

HEY, ARATA, WE'RE ALMOST AT THE RENDEZVOUS POINT WITH THE FREEDOM FIGHTERS.

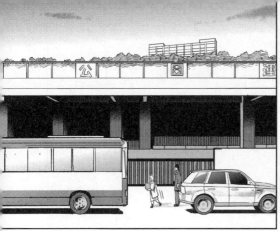

WAVE
サッ

BOW
ペコ

PER-FECT.

THAT'S EVERY-THING.

WHAT?

?

HUH?

LET'S TEST...

くる
TURN

NOW THEN,

スッ
STARE

EXCUSE ME?

THE ENDS GOT BURNT SO I HAD NO CHOICE.

OH, MY HAIR? I CUT IT YESTERDAY.

THE HECK...

グ ッ FWIP

OH YEAH! I QUIT MY JOB!

YOU'RE GOING TO BE LEAVING JAPAN, RIGHT, ARATA?

I MEAN, THERE WAS NO POINT IN STAYING AT THAT COMPANY ANY LONGER NOW THAT I'VE MET YOU AGAIN.

もじ FIDGET  もじ FIDGET  もじ FIDGET

146

WHAT DO YOU MEAN "WHY NOT!?" BECAUSE IT'S DANGEROUS, OBVIOUSLY! THERE'S NO WAY I CAN GET MY FRIENDS INVOLVED IN SOMETHING LIKE THIS!

WHY NOT!?

IF MY BOY-FRIEND IS IN DANGER...

THEN I'LL FIGHT WITH YOU!

ERR... YEAH, WE ARE... BUT WE'RE GOING TO GO BEAT UP A CRIME SYNDICATE FIRST.

WHAT? NOT A CHANCE.

THEN IT'S MY JOB

TO GO SAVE HIM!

AH...

MISS SOPHIA?

.....

TURN
くる...

NO PROB-LEM!

AND WE DON'T OFFER A SALARY.

OUR JOB'S PRETTY DANGER-OUS.

WELL, WE DO NEED MORE FIGHTING POWER, SO...

HUH?

THERE'S A HUGE PROB-LEM!

ぱあ...

SPARKLE

UMM...

IT'S NOT?

OMAR, THAT REALLY ISN'T THE ISSUE HERE.

·····

STAND

ス...

DUMBFOUNDED!

AND WE'VE GOT PLENTY OF SPARE CROSS-BOWS LEFT OVER NOW.

SHE'LL PROBABLY BE USEFUL TO HAVE AROUND.

WHAT?

AFTER SEEING HER FIGHT YESTERDAY, I HAVE TO ADMIT... SHE'S PRETTY GOOD WITH A CROSS-BOW.

AHH...

ARATA.

PLEASE...

WELCOME ABOARD, MISS SOPHIA.

THANK YOU!

OKAY...

IT'S ALMOST TIME.

TO ACTIVATE YOUR I-ILLUMINATOR TRACKERS,

I WANT YOU ALL

BUT THERE'S NOTHING WE CAN DO ABOUT THAT.

GRIN

WE'VE GOT A NEW ADDITION TO OUR TEAM, AND WE HAVEN'T HAD TIME TO MAKE ANY PREPARATIONS.

BEEP

BEEP

BEEP

Complete

BEEP

THE I-ILLU-MINATOR'S INFO LINK IS COMPLETE.

TACTICAL UNIT P IS READY FOR DEPLOY-MENT.

HISSSSS

ALL SQUADS, MOVE OUT.

OKAY, LET'S TAKE THIS NICE AND SLOW.

JUMP

JIBRIL, IT'S NICE THAT YOU FOUND A SHORTCUT, BUT THERE'S NO NEED TO HURRY.

ROGER, SORRY.

NOT— AH, DO YOU MIND IF WE STAND OUT A LITTLE?

VRRRR

JINI, IS THERE ANY WAY YOUR SQUAD CAN MOVE FASTER?

HM? AS LONG AS IT'S NOT TOO MUCH, SURE.

STEP

GRAB

DASH

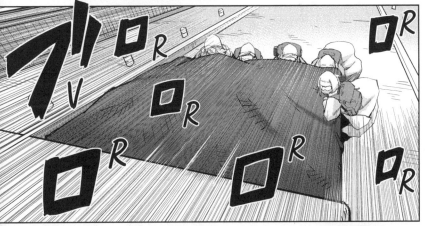

IT'S LIKE YOU CAN SEE EXACTLY WHAT'S GOING ON. DO YOU KNOW WHAT KIND OF FACE I'M MAKING RIGHT NOW, TOO?

GRIT

IT'S GOOD THAT YOU'RE MOVING FASTER, BUT DON'T USE THAT TRANS-PORTATION METHOD FOR TOO LONG.

AH... THEY MUST HAVE GRABBED ONTO A TRUCK OR SOME-THING.

40 KM/H?

MAYBE, MAYBE NOT. IT'S A SECRET.

ARATA, WE'LL REACH OUR DESTINATION IN 60 SECONDS.

GOT-CHA.

THE FIRST WAREHOUSE HAS BEEN BOMBED,

BOOM

CLINK

I REALLY HOPE NO ONE GETS HURT...

THANK-FULLY THERE'S NOT TOO MANY PEDES-TRIANS.

BOOM!

TOSS

AND... THREE.

BANG!

BANG!

SUP-PRES-SION COM-PLETE.

PHEW.

WE WANT TO THIN THE ENEMY'S NUM-BERS AS MUCH AS POSSI-BLE.

SQUAT

ALL SQUADS, START FIRING ON ANY TACTICAL UNITS YOU FIND.

THERE ARE ONLY SIX LEFT... THIS IS GOOD PROG-RESS.

WE'VE DES-TROYED 12 WARE-HOUSES.

**Targets Destroyed**

12/18

TELL HIM I'D LIKE TO HAVE A LITTLE *CHAT.*

NOW THEN, I WANT YOU TO CONTACT YOUR BOSS FOR ME.

YOU WON'T DIE FROM THOSE WOUNDS.

DON'T WORRY.

CLICK

WE'LL SLAUGHTER EVERYONE HE CARES ABOUT, FROM HIS FAMILY TO HIS MISTRESS.

TELL HIM IF HE DOESN'T COME BY THEN...

IF YOU DON'T CONTACT HIM IN THAT TIME, YOU'RE DEAD.

I'LL GIVE YOU FIVE MINUTES.

コツ
NOD

UNDER-STOOD?

AM I

E

**Preparing for Combat**

↑

SE

IF THAT'S WHAT IT TAKES TO PROTECT THOSE KIDS, I'LL GLADLY BECOME A VILLAIN.

STAND
ス

YOU'VE GOTTEN PRETTY GOOD AT PLAYING THE BAD GUY.

I'LL SEND SD TO REINFORCE YOU. ONCE THEY'VE NEUTRAL-IZED THE BUILDING, RESUME YOUR ASSAULT.

SPLIT UP AND HIDE BEHIND THE COR-NERS OF THE BUILD-ING.

SE, STOP YOUR ASSAULT AND TAKE COVER. YOU'RE OUTNUM-BERED.

AT THE FIRST AND SECOND FLOOR WINDOWS.

I WANT YOU TO LOB ALL YOUR GRE-NADES AND MOLO-TOVS

LOOK OUT THE WINDOW. DO YOU SEE THE BUILDING AT YOUR TWO?

SD.

PHEW.

NOW THEN...

NOT A PROB-LEM.

DASH

WE'LL NEED 20 SECONDS TO PRE-PARE.

DASH

ARATA!

SOPHIE? WHAT IS IT?

GRANTED, THEY PROBABLY WON'T STORM THE BUILDING RIGHT AWAY, SO WE'VE GOT A LITTLE BIT MORE TIME THAN THAT.

WE SET UP TRAFFIC JAMS ON BOTH SIDES, BUT THE POLICE WILL STILL GET HERE IN ABOUT FIVE MINUTES.

I CAN'T ALLOW YOU TO FIGHT AN UNKNOWN FOE. WHAT INFORMATION DO YOU HAVE ON IT!?

UMM...

BUT IT'S HEADED STRAIGHT FOR YOU!

WHAT DO YOU MEAN, WEIRD? ANYWAY, DON'T ENGAGE AND KEEP YOUR DISTANCE.

TH-THERE'S SOMETHING WEIRD HEADING YOUR WAY!

THEY'RE HEAVILY ARMED, AND THEY'RE COVERED FROM HEAD TO TOE IN PROTECTIVE GEAR!

THERE'S TWO OF THEM... AND THEY'VE GOT THESE WEIRD IRON POLES STRAPPED TO THE SIDES OF THEIR BODIES!

CLINK

CLINK

‼️

BANG

BANG

BANG

SC

E

E

SA

SC, CAN YOU SNIPE THEM?

WE'LL TRY.

CLINK

CLINK

RAISE

I'D NEED TO SEE THEM MYSELF, BUT... IF MAUSERS AREN'T WORKING, THEN THEY'RE DEFINITELY DANGEROUS.

ANY IDEA HOW TO DEAL WITH THEM?

THE MAUSERS CAN'T PENETRATE THEIR ARMOR!

RA TA TA

TA TA

IT'S NO GOOD!

RA TA TA TA TA TA

JIBRIL, THAT'S ENOUGH.

BEGIN YOUR RE- TREAT.

HERE TO PARLEY? YEAH.

DOESN'T LOOK LIKE THEY'RE—

CLICK

SEE IF A GRENADE-TIPPED ARROW CAN GET THROUGH.

ROGER.

SOPHIE, YOU'RE BEHIND THEM, RIGHT?

SC

E E

YEAH.

SA

BOOM!

. . . . .

THE ARROWS PENETRATED THEIR ARMOR, SO WE MIGHT NOT HAVE EVEN NEEDED THE GRENADES.

TARGET ELIMINATED... UGH, THEY'RE MISSING THEIR TORSOS NOW.

I SEE. WELL DONE. BEGIN YOUR RETREAT.

HAVE ALL THE SQUADS RETREAT.

IBN, JINI, I THINK WE'VE DONE ENOUGH DAMAGE TO OUR FOE.

STEP

ガタン RATTLE...

YOU GUYS SURE MADE A MESS OF THINGS.

OH MAN...

I HOPE YOU'RE HERE TO TALK.

GOOD EVENING.

SMIRK

AHA HAHA HAHA HA!

DIDN'T YOU SAY YOU NEVER WANTED TO SEE US AGAIN?

YA DAMN LIAR!

SCRAPE

THAT WAS, THEN, THIS IS NOW.

ANYWAY, WHY DON'T YOU COME TAKE A SEAT?

WE CAN'T HAVE A PROPER CONVER-SATION IF YOU'RE ALL STANDING NOW, CAN WE?

JUST TO MAKE SURE...

YOU'RE FROM THE CULT...

AND YOU'RE FROM THE CRIME SYNDICATE, CORRECT?

OPERATION_029
## RETURNING OVERSEAS

YOU WON'T EVER BE ABLE TO DO BUSINESS IN THIS TOWN NOW.

THIS IS OVER-KILL...

YOU SCARED THIS GUY'S BOSS SHIT-LESS, SO HE SENT HIS SECOND-IN-COMMAND.

YEAH.

.....

YOU SEEM TO BE MIS-UNDER-STANDING SOME-THING.

WE WERE NEVER INTER-ESTED IN DOING BUSI-NESS IN THE FIRST PLACE.

I TOLD YOU, YAN-SAN. THESE GUYS DON'T CARE ABOUT TURF WARS AND THE LIKE. THEY'RE HONEST TO GOODNESS MERCENARIES.

IT'S AS HE SAYS.

WHY ARE YOU DOING ALL THIS?

THEN...

I IMAGINE YOU'RE ALREADY AWARE, BUT WE'LL BE LEAVING THE COUNTRY TOMORROW.

OUR GOAL IS SOLELY TO SECURE SAFE PASSAGE FOR OURSELVES.

AHAHAHA! YOU HEAR THAT, KAJITA!? THEY SAID THEY'RE DOING THIS FOR THEIR OWN SAFETY!

THESE GUYS ARE CRAZY ENOUGH TO START A WAR JUST TO SECURE SAFE PASSAGE!

PFFT

IF YOU ASK ME, YOU'RE BOTH FUCKING INSANE.

• • • • •

MERCE-NARIES ARE WAY CRAZIER THAN CULTISTS.

OH MAN.

FAIR ENOUGH.

BUT IF WE HADN'T ATTACKED YOU, WE BOTH KNOW YOU WOULD HAVE TRIED TO TAKE REVENGE AGAINST US.

SO WE HAD TO TAKE PRECAU-TIONS.

SAY WHAT YOU WANT.

I'VE GOTTA SAY THOUGH, YOU REALLY DON'T HALF-ASS THINGS. YOUR "PRECAU-TIONS" HAVE PRACTICALLY DESTROYED YAN-SAN'S BUSINESS.

OUR MONKS ARE STILL IN FIGHTING SHAPE.

HOW-EVER...

HEY, MERCE-NARY.

I'D SAY YOUR ACTIONS THIS TIME AROUND HAVE CREATED QUITE A FEW GRUDGES.

TWITCH

IF YOU KEEP THIRSTING FOR REVENGE,

YOU WON'T BE ABLE TO MAKE ANY MONEY.

OH, I'M WELL AWARE OF THAT.

BUT YOU KNOW...

.....

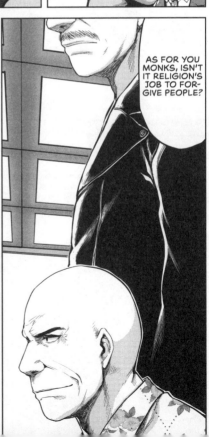

AS FOR YOU MONKS, ISN'T IT RELIGION'S JOB TO FORGIVE PEOPLE?

WHAT THE HELL...

ARE YOU GUYS!?

175

SO IF YOU'RE LOOKING FOR SOMEONE TO BLAME FOR THE INCIDENT AT KAWA-SAKI OR EVEN THIS ATTACK, YOU'RE BARKING UP THE WRONG TREE.

WE ONLY TARGETED YOU GUYS BECAUSE THE GOVERNMENT HIRED US TO.

JUST TO SET THE RECORD STRAIGHT.

I ONLY REALIZED THIS RECENTLY, BUT I THINK THE GOVERNMENT WANTED AN EXCUSE TO GET THE NATIONAL POLICE FORCE INVOLVED WITH THIS CITY.

IF I WERE YOU, I'D TRY TO FLEE BEFORE IT'S TOO LATE. OH, AND I RE-COMMEND HIDING YOUR ASSETS BEFORE THEY GET SEIZED.

WHY...

WHY DID THE GOVERN-MENT HIRE YOU GUYS INSTEAD OF GOING TO THE POLICE?

YOU BAS- TARDS!

DO YOU KNOW HOW MANY PEOPLE DIED BECAUSE OF YOU!?

SO THIS WAS ALL TO GIVE THE POLICE A PRE- TEXT TO INTER- VENE.

I SEE...

I KNOW I DON'T.

WELL, I'M SURE YOU DON'T WANT ANY MORE DEATHS TONIGHT.

WA—

I CAN'T PROMISE ANY- THING.

.....

WHAT A SHAME.

THR

WAIT!

ガタ RATTLE

IF YOU JUST LET US LEAVE IN PEACE, WE CAN PUT ALL OF THIS BEHIND US.

WHAT ABOUT YOU GUYS?

A WISE DECISION.

I...

I PROMISE WE'LL BACK OFF.

WELL...

PERHAPS.

THAT'S WHY I CAME HERE TO NEGOTIATE.

I BET MY BOYS COULD GIVE YOUR KIDS A RUN FOR THEIR MONEY.

EVEN IF WE WOULDN'T COME OUT UNSCATHED,

DIPLO-MACY ISN'T MY STRONG SUIT.

THIS IS SOME PRETTY SHITTY NEGO-TIATING.

NOT AT ALL. HALF OUR CLIENTS DEFAULT ON THEIR PAYMENTS.

BY THE WAY, IS IT PROFIT-ABLE, BEING A MERCENARY?

HM? IF IT DOESN'T MAKE YOU MONEY, WHY DO YOU DO IT?

YOU THINK A MONK COULD MAKE IT AS A MERCE-NARY?

•••••

IF IT WAS JUST ABOUT GETTING RICH, IT'D PROBABLY MAKE MORE SENSE TO JOIN A SYNDICATE SOMEWHERE.

BECAUSE THIS IS THE ONLY THING I'M GOOD AT, AND I DON'T WANT TO BECOME A CRIMINAL.

I SEE.

MERCENARIES WHO'RE WILLING TO INCUR CIVILIAN CASUALTIES

AREN'T VERY POPULAR.

IT CAN'T BE THAT HARD IF EVEN SOMEONE LIKE ME CAN MANAGE IT.

PROBABLY.

HOWEVER...

DON'T YOU DARE—

HEY!

WHO SLAUGHTER INNOCENT WOMEN AND CHILDREN.

ESPECIALLY ONES

KAJITA.

HE'S JUST GIVING ADVICE.

WE SHOULD TAKE IT.

BUT SHUWASAN...

ANYWAY.

WE DON'T HAVE MUCH TIME LEFT BEFORE THE COPS ARRIVE.

SO LET'S WRAP THINGS UP.

PAT

.....

AND WHAT'S THAT?

BUT THERE'S SOMETHING I WANT TO DISCUSS FIRST.

WE'LL PROMISE NOT TO MESS WITH YOU GUYS...

WHEN YOU GUYS LEAVE THE COUNTRY TOMOR-ROW,

DO YOU THINK YOU COULD TAKE US ALONG?

THAT SHOULD BE POS-SIBLE.

HOW MANY OF YOUR GUYS WILL YOU BE BRING-ING?

ITOU-SAN'S AGENCY PROBABLY WANTS TO WASH THEIR HANDS OF THESE GUYS ASAP, TOO.

IT'S NOT A BAD PRO-POSAL...

LET ME THINK...

.....

THE REST'LL WANT TO STAY IN JAPAN.

MAYBE AROUND FOUR OR FIVE.

IT SEEMS WE HAVE A DEAL.

IN RETURN FOR SMUGGLING FOUR TO FIVE OF YOUR MEN OUT OF THE COUNTRY,

YOU AGREE NOT TO LAY A HAND ON MY KIDS, CORRECT?

YEAH.

. . . . .

UNDER-STOOD.

I'LL DO MY BEST TO NEGOTIATE YOUR SAFE PASSAGE.

WELL, WE'VE SECURED OUR SAFETY FOR NOW,

AND OUR CLIENT HAS GOTTEN US A FLIGHT FOR TO-MORROW.

ON SECOND THOUGHT,

LET'S JUST TALK ABOUT THIS LATER.

HONESTLY, I'VE GOT NO CLUE WHAT THE SITUATION THERE IS, SO WE'LL HAVE TO START BY...

WE'LL BE GOING TO THAILAND, IT SEEMS.

GRAB
ヒョ

MOST OF THE KIDS HAVE GOTTEN USED TO USING CHOP-STICKS NOW.

HM? OH, YEAH,

AH, UHH...

JUST A FEW DAYS AGO, THEY WERE STILL EATING WITH THEIR HANDS AND GETTING GREASE EVERY-WHERE.

THEY'RE PRETTY QUICK ON THE UPTAKE.

Ha Ha Ha Ha

I'M STILL PRAC-TICING MYSELF.

STOP RIGHT THERE!

CLINK

WELL, I KNOW SOME-ONE WHO MIGHT CARE.

HMM.

MUTTER

WHO CARES WHAT I USE, AS LONG AS IT WORKS?

YOU'RE SUPPOSED TO EAT JAPANESE FOOD WITH CHOPSTICKS.

I BET HE LIKES PEOPLE WHO TRY THEIR BEST TO LEARN ABOUT JAPANESE CULTURE.

MUTTER

DON'T FORGET, ARATA'S FROM JAPAN.

NOT EVEN CLOSE!

MASTER, IS THIS HOW I HOLD THEM!?

.....

BACK THEN...

I WAS THE ONLY PERSON SHE EVER TALKED TO. BUT NOW...

HEY.

JIBRIL.

CHEW

もぐ もぐ

CHEW

FOR REAL!?

SLIDE

SLIDE

SLIDE

SPIT

DID YOU MAKE HIM FALL FOR YOU!?

UM... YES.

CHEW
もぐ

DID YOU WEAR THE MAID OUTFIT IN FRONT OF HIM?

もぐ
CHEW

もぐ
CHEW

GUESS NOT.

.....

SHAKE
ふる

SHAKE
ふる

WHAT'RE THOSE?

GLIMMER

JIBRIL! BACK WHEN WE INFILTRATED THE MAID CAFE, I LEARNED SOMETHING ELSE ABOUT JAPAN! APPARENTLY THERE ARE THESE THINGS CALLED SCHOOL SWIMSUITS.

IT'S A TYPE OF CLOTHING!

I THINK IT DID HELP A LITTLE,

BUT...

ぱぁ...
SPARKLE

WE MADE ROMANOV TRY IT LAST NIGHT.

DON'T WORRY, I GOT ONE AHEAD OF TIME.

BUT WE'RE LEAVING JAPAN TOMORROW, THERE'S NO TIME TO BUY MORE...

IT WAS UHH... PRETTY GOOD.

WHEN DID SHE FIND THE TIME TO DO THAT...

GRIN ニ9

GRIN ニ9

NO, NO, NO!

IN THAT CASE... MAYBE I...

NO! THRICE AS EFFECTIVE!

WAHAHA!

IF THE MAID OUTFIT WORKED A LITTLE, THEN THE SCHOOL SWIMSUIT WILL BE TWICE AS EFFECTIVE!

WAHAHA!

WAHAHA!

•••••

Y-YEAH! IT'S OKAY! WE WON'T LET THAT BLONDE-HAIRED ELF BEAT YOU!

DON'T WORRY! ONCE YOU WEAR THAT SCHOOL SWIMSUIT, YOU'LL BE INVINCIBLE!

DO—

.....

I...

SIGN: TOUR BUS

I'M JUST GLAD I GOT TO MEET ARATA AGAIN.

. . . . .

OH, I DIDN'T MEAN IT IN A BAD WAY, HONESTLY, I THOUGHT THE TEMPURA WAS GREAT.

SORRY.

THAT CERTAINLY WAS ONE EVENTFUL VACATION.

MMM.

THINGS ENDED UP GETTING MORE HECTIC THAN I PLANNED.

SORRY, EVERY- ONE.

IT'S OKAY.

BECAUSE IN THE END, WE STILL WON!

LOOKING FOR SOMEONE?

NOW THEN... WE NEED OUR TICKETS, BUT I DON'T SEE ITOU-SAN ANYWHERE.

YEAH, THEY REALLY HATE TO LOSE.

NOTHING... I WAS JUST THINKING YOU ALWAYS HAVE IMPECCABLE TIMING.

THANK YOU VERY MUCH.

.....

WHAT'S WRONG?

I BELIEVE YOU'LL NEED THESE.

IT'D BE HORRIBLE IF SOMETHING LIKE THIS HAPPENED IN JAPAN AGAIN.

WELL, DO A BETTER JOB OF CONTROLLING THEM NEXT TIME.

THE PEOPLE SHOULD BE ABLE TO ENJOY DREAMING IN PEACE.

WHAT'S IMPORTANT ISN'T CRUSHING YOUR ENEMIES,

BUT RATHER, EFFECTIVELY CONTROLLING THEM.

WE CAN SPREAD RUMORS THAT YOUR HIT WAS A SPECIAL OPERATION LED BY THE GOVERNMENT, WHICH SHOULD KEEP THE OTHER CRIMINAL ORGANIZATIONS IN LINE.

REGARDLESS, WE'LL BE ABLE TO MAKE GOOD USE OF THE COMMOTION YOU CAUSED.

INDEED, WHO KNOWS HOW MANY PEOPLE LIKE YOU ARE LYING DORMANT IN THIS COUNTRY.

BAD THINGS HAPPEN IF YOU WAKE THEM FROM THEIR SLUMBER.

· · · ·

WHAT'S THIS?

HERE YOU GO.

BUT IN THE END, YOU DID REMOVE TWO OF JAPAN'S BIGGEST THREATS.

AFTER THE SCENE YOU CAUSED, I WASN'T SURE IF I SHOULD GIVE THIS TO YOU OR NOT...

THINK OF IT AS THE ADVANCE PAYMENT WE SHOULD HAVE GIVEN YOU WHEN YOU SIGNED THE CONTRACT.

YOUR REWARD.

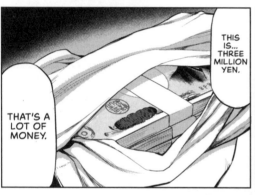

THIS IS... THREE MILLION YEN.

THAT'S A LOT OF MONEY.

YOU EARNED IT. NOW THEN, I MUST BE GOING...

AH, WAIT!

THAT SHE DOESN'T NEED TO TRY SO HARD TO FAKE ALL THOSE BOMBASTIC PERSONALITIES.

PLEASE TELL THAT YOUNG OPERATIVE OF YOURS

HER PERSONALITY WAS BUILT AROUND THE DATA WE COLLECTED ON YOUR PREFERENCES BACK WHEN YOU STILL LIVED IN JAPAN.

BUT IT SEEMS SHE FAILED TO SELL THE ACT.

FAREWELL.

ITOU-SAN.

NAH, IT WASN'T A FAILURE, I HAD A LOT OF FUN TALKING TO YOU...

STAND
スッ

. . . . .

OH, I DON'T SEE KAJITA-SAN ANYWHERE.

YO, MERC.

UMM... YOUR NAME IS SHUWA-SAN, RIGHT?

YEP, THAT'S ME.

HE LOVES JAPAN TOO MUCH TO LEAVE.

I SEE...

WHAT DO YOU SAY TO ADDING US TO YOUR GROUP?

I'M NOT INTERESTED IN LOOKING AFTER ADULTS.

WOW, YOU REALLY DO ONLY HAVE KIDS WITH YOU.

SOUNDS GOOD.

OUR PLANE'S GOING TO THAILAND, BY THE WAY.

A FEW EXTRA PEOPLE CAN'T HURT.

COME ON, THERE'S ONLY FOUR OF US.

IF YOU COME WITH ME, YOU WON'T BE GETTING A SALARY.

*AHAHAHA!* FAIR ENOUGH!

BUT THAT WAS THEN, THIS IS NOW. BESIDES, WE'RE HEADED TO THE SAME PLACE ANYWAY!

I CAN'T BELIEVE YOU'RE SAYING THAT WHEN WE WERE TRYING TO KILL EACH OTHER LESS THAN 24 HOURS AGO.

WHY THE SUDDEN CHANGE OF HEART?

ARE THEY SERIOUSLY PLANNING ON JOINING US?

WELL...

SO MUCH FOR SIGHT-SEEING.

.....

I HOPE

THIS TRIP MANAGED TO TEACH THEM JUST A LITTLE BIT OF WHAT IT'S LIKE TO LIVE A NORMAL LIFE.

HUH?

WHAT'D YOU DO?

PLEASE GET MAD AT ME, I DID SOMETHING BAD.

ARATA,

.....

SHE'S TALKING ABOUT SOPHIE, ISN'T SHE?

LET THE EVIL DJINN JOIN US.

I...

I UNDER-ESTIMATED HER.

THAT'S NOT IT.

IT'S FINE.

YOU MADE THE RATIONAL CALL. PLUS, SHE DEFINITELY SAVED OUR HIDES IN THAT LAST FIGHT.

THE IT'S JOB TO G SAVE HIM!

DIDN'T WANT YOU GIVING HER SPECIAL TREAT-MENT.

WHAT DO YOU MEAN "WHY NOT!?" BECAUSE IT'S DANGEROUS, OBVIOUSLY! THERE'S NO WAY I CAN GET MY FRIENDS INVOLVED IN SOMETHING LIKE THIS!

WHY NOT!?

THEN I FI W Y

BACK THEN...

I...

THAT'S WHY I WANTED HER TO JOIN.

IF MY BOY-FRIEND IS IN DANGER.

WHAT? NOT A CHANCE.

SO PLEASE... GET MAD AT ME.

I'M A BAD PERSON.

YOU'RE JUST HUMAN.

THAT'S NOT TRUE.

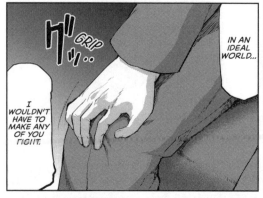

GRIP

IN AN IDEAL WORLD...

I WOULDN'T HAVE TO MAKE ANY OF YOU FIGHT.

IN...

SLOWLY

BUT SURELY...

.....

I'M GOING TO WIN

A BETTER FUTURE FOR ALL OF YOU.

I SEE. YOU SISTERS DID A PRETTY GOOD JOB, HUH?

IT'S KOJIMA.

WHO CARES WHAT NAME I CALL YOU?

OH PLEASE, THAT'S PROBABLY AN ALIAS TOO.

MORE IMPORTANTLY, WHEN IS THE HEADMASTER LANDING?

SIGN: WOMEN'S

PLEASE TAKE GOOD CARE OF THEM.

THEY'LL ARRIVE IN SUVARNABHUMI AIRPORT IN ANOTHER 5 HOURS AND 40 MINUTES.

TAKE CARE OF THEM?

BESIDES,

THERE'S SOMETHING I'VE ALWAYS WANTED TO TRY IF I GOT TO MEET THE HEADMASTER.

I MAY RESPECT YOUR OPINION, BUT YOU HAVE NO INFLUENCE HERE.

I'LL USE THEM HOW I SEE FIT. NOTHING MORE, NOTHING LESS.

I'M LOOKING FORWARD TO SEEING

HOW HE HANDLES IT...

# MARGINAL OPERATION 5 : END
## TO BE CONTINUED IN VOLUME 6

# STAFF

STORY WRITER
**Yuri Shibamura**

MANGA ILLUSTRATOR
**Daisuke Kimura**

SETTING ASSISTANCE
**Shizuma Yoshinori**

BACKGROUNDS AND TONING
**Shin Moriyama**

BACKGROUNDS
**Maho Tsuchiya**

3D MAP DESIGN
**Akito Ootsuka**

EDITING
**Yutaka Kawamura**

DESIGN
**Jun Kawana** (prigraphics)

SPECIAL THANKS
**Syuji Imada**
**Jun Kimura**

PRESIDENT AND PUBLISHER
**Samuel Pinansky**

MANAGING EDITOR (MANGA)
**J. Collis**

MANAGING TRANSLATOR
**Kristi Fernandez**

MARKETING MANAGER
**Stephanie Hii**

TRANSLATION
**Ningen**

EDITING AND LETTERING
**Meiru**

The events recorded in this
manga are based off of the state of the
world in the time it was written.

MARGINAL OPERATION (MANGA) VOLUME 5
by Yuri Shibamura (story) and Daisuke Kimura (artwork)

First published in Japan in 2016 by Kodansha Ltd., Tokyo.
Publication rights for this English edition arranged through Kodansha Ltd., Tokyo.

Find more books like this one at www.j-novel.club!

ISBN: 978-1-7183-5904-8
Printed in Korea
First Printing: March 2021
10 9 8 7 6 5 4 3 2 1

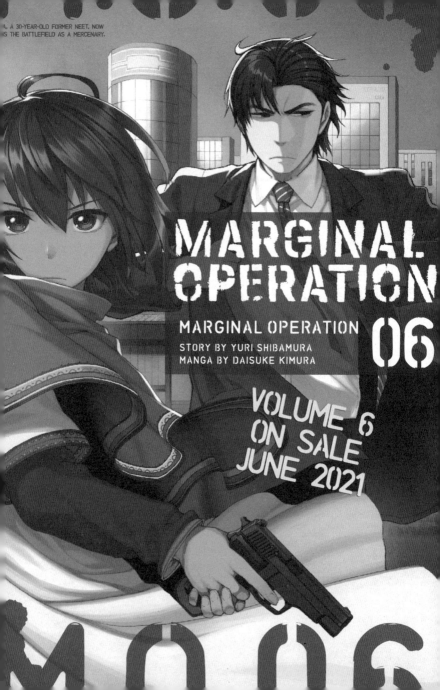

ASCENDANCE
OF A
BOOKWORM
I'll do anything to
become a librarian!

Part 1 **If there aren't any
books, I'll just have
to make some! IV**

Author: **Miya Kazuki** / Artist: **Suzuka**
Character Designer: **You Shiina**

VOLUME 4
ON SALE NOW!

# How a Realist Hero

# Rebuilt the Kingdom

I

**MANGA OMNIBUS 1 ON SALE NOW!**

Manga ✛ Satoshi Ueda
Original Work ✛ Dojyomaru
Original Character Design ✛ Fuyuyuki

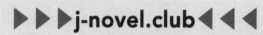

# J-Novel Club Lineup

## Ebook Releases Series List

A Lily Blooms in Another World
A Wild Last Boss Appeared!
Altina the Sword Princess
Amagi Brilliant Park
An Archdemon's Dilemma:
   How to Love Your Elf Bride
Arifureta Zero
Arifureta: From Commonplace
   to World's Strongest
Ascendance of a Bookworm
Beatless
Bibliophile Princess
Black Summoner
By the Grace of the Gods
Campfire Cooking in Another
   World with My Absurd Skill
Can Someone Please Explain
   What's Going On?!
Cooking with Wild Game
Crest of the Stars
Deathbound Duke's Daughter
Demon Lord, Retry!
Der Werwolf: The Annals of Veight
From Truant to Anime Screenwriter:
   My Path to "Anohana" and "The
   Anthem of the Heart"
Full Metal Panic!
Grimgar of Fantasy and Ash
Her Majesty's Swarm
Holmes of Kyoto
How a Realist Hero Rebuilt the
   Kingdom
How NOT to Summon a Demon
   Lord
I Refuse to Be Your Enemy!
I Saved Too Many Girls and Caused
   the Apocalypse
I Shall Survive Using Potions!
In Another World With My
   Smartphone
Infinite Dendrogram
Infinite Stratos
Invaders of the Rokujouma!?
Isekai Rebuilding Project
JK Haru is a Sex Worker in Another
   World
Kobold King
Kokoro Connect
Last and First Idol
Lazy Dungeon Master
Mapping: The Trash-Tier Skill That
   Got Me Into a Top-Tier Party

Middle-Aged Businessman, Arise in
   Another World!
Mixed Bathing in Another
   Dimension
Monster Tamer
My Big Sister Lives in a Fantasy
   World
My Instant Death Ability is So
   Overpowered, No One in This
   Other World Stands a Chance
   Against Me!
My Next Life as a Villainess: All
   Routes Lead to Doom!
Otherside Picnic
Outbreak Company
Outer Ragna
Record of Wortenia War
Seirei Gensouki: Spirit Chronicles
Sexiled: My Sexist Party Leader
   Kicked Me Out, So I Teamed Up
   With a Mythical Sorceress!
Slayers
Sorcerous Stabber Orphen:
   The Wayward Journey
Tearmoon Empire
Teogonia
The Bloodline
The Combat Butler and Automaton
   Waitress
The Economics of Prophecy
The Epic Tale of the Reincarnated
   Prince Herscherik
The Extraordinary, the Ordinary,
   and SOAP!
The Greatest Magicmaster's
   Retirement Plan
The Holy Knight's Dark Road
The Magic in this Other World is
   Too Far Behind!
The Master of Ragnarok & Blesser
   of Einherjar
The Sorcerer's Receptionist
The Tales of Marielle Clarac
The Underdog of the Eight Greater
   Tribes
The Unwanted Undead Adventurer
WATARU!!! The Hot-Blooded
   Fighting Teen & His Epic
   Adventures in a Fantasy World
   After Stopping a Truck with His
   Bare Hands!!

The White Cat's Revenge as
   Plotted from the Demon King's
   Lap
The World's Least Interesting
   Master Swordsman
Welcome to Japan, Ms. Elf!
When the Clock Strikes Z
Wild Times with a Fake Fake
   Princess

### Manga Series:

A Very Fairy Apartment
An Archdemon's Dilemma:
   How to Love Your Elf Bride
Animeta!
Ascendance of a Bookworm
Bibliophile Princess
Black Summoner
Campfire Cooking in Another
   World with My Absurd Skill
Cooking with Wild Game
Demon Lord, Retry!
Discommunication
How a Realist Hero Rebuilt the
   Kingdom
I Love Yuri and I Got Bodyswapped
   with a Fujoshi!
I Shall Survive Using Potions!
Infinite Dendrogram
Mapping: The Trash-Tier Skill That
   Got Me Into a Top-Tier Party
Marginal Operation
Record of Wortenia War
Seirei Gensouki: Spirit Chronicles
Sorcerous Stabber Orphen:
   The Reckless Journey
Sorcerous Stabber Orphen:
   The Youthful Journey
Sweet Reincarnation
The Faraway Paladin
The Magic in this Other World is
   Too Far Behind!
The Master of Ragnarok & Blesser
   of Einherjar
The Tales of Marielle Clarac
The Unwanted Undead Adventurer

Keep an eye out at j-novel.club
   for further new title
   announcements!